Written from a pastor's hea... *Flourish*... ...e, and pro-
found depiction of the pow... found... ...d's house.
Pastor Lee hits the nail on th... ...e head, ...n that the
environment around us acti... ...ates the destiny ... ...and discover the
life that God intends you to live—one of nourishing in the courts of God, full
of purpose, passion, and provision.

—LISA BEVERE
New York Times best-selling author and speaker

Choosing to just get by in life is one of the greatest enemies to the church.
If you look at Scripture, you'll actually see a strong opposition to living
apathetically—you'll see that we were designed by God to flourish. I'm
grateful that my good friend Lee Cummings wrote this book to help us move
past the noise and static of confusion, exhaustion, and hopelessness. *Flourish* is
full of key insights that will help lead you out of a life of survival and into one
of thriving. Get ready to experience an upgrade in your spiritual life!

—ERIC JOHNSON
Senior Pastor, Bethel Church

I am grateful that my friend Lee Cummings wrote a book on the subject
of flourishing. It's God's desire for each one of us to grow and develop in a
healthy and vigorous way, experiencing the full goodness of God. Yet many
people find that their lives do not appear to manifest the full picture of His
goodness and grace, and often feel stagnant or uncertain about what to do
next. In this book, Lee has done a brilliant job of unpacking what it takes
to experience a life of thriving. With the heart of a pastor and the voice of a
prophet, he invites us on a journey that leads us to settling for nothing less
than the complete manifestation of God's desires for us.

—BANNING LIEBSCHER
Founder and Pastor, Jesus Culture

Lee calls us to sink our roots deeply into the rich soil of a healthy local church
because it's the garden where we truly flourish. Read this book prayerfully,
and you'll begin to feel Jesus's jealous passion for the church He's building.

—BOB SORGE
Author, *Secrets of the Secret Place*

In a world that beats you up, God wants to build you up. God has done something wonderful for you, is doing something wonderful in you, and has plans
to do something wonderful through you. This book from my friend Pastor Lee
Cummings is a helpful, practical, biblical resource to help you experience the
goodness of God and greatness of life with God.

—MARK DRISCOLL
Founding Senior Pastor, The Trinity Church
President, Mark Driscoll Ministries

Have you ever wondered how you fit into the family of God? In this book, my
friend Lee Cummings shares revelatory truths about how we, as children of
God, can live a flourishing life in the courts of God. This book is a must-read

for anyone who wants to know more about the power and purpose of God in their life.

—ROBERT MORRIS
Lead Senior Pastor, Gateway Church
Best-selling author, *The Blessed Life, Frequency,* and
Beyond Blessed

The soil in which our life is rooted and the spiritual environment in which we live will directly impact our spiritual health and growth. In his book *Flourish*, Lee Cummings speaks to the soil of the church and the spiritual environment that every believer must dwell in to live a flourishing life—a life that allows us to grow into our full potential and purpose in God. This is a challenging and encouraging exposé of what those seeking God's work in their lives must know and apply.

—TOM LANE
Apostolic Senior Pastor, Gateway Church

I am blown away by Lee's new book! He is one of the sharpest minds I know. I have read *Flourish* from cover to cover, and I am thrilled by what Lee has captured in this amazing book. It is packed with truths that are hard-hitting and convincing. I challenge you to read this book in its entirety.

—RICK RENNER
Author, minister, and television broadcaster
Moscow, Russia

Books that matter, the kind that change people's lives, are written out of life experiences that are tested and proven true. Lee has cared for the people and communities surrounding his church for decades, teaching and preaching the Word of God in a way that empowers people to hope that the promises of God are true and within reach for everyone. In *Flourish*, Lee lays a foundation for people to gain an unshakeable identity in Christ, a legitimate place in the loving family of God, a Spirit-empowered anointing for specific divine assignments, and ongoing supernatural provision to thrive in a world that seeks to deplete individual destinies. You will feel inspired and challenged as Lee blends real-world life experiences with the Word of God to encourage any person, any Christian leader, anyone answering the call of God to step into the promises of God and flourish!

—DR. NATE RUCH
Lead Pastor, Emmanuel Christian Center

Pastor Lee is a contemporary theologian with a mastery of biblical truth and a unique understanding of current, cultural realities. *Flourish* is a great example of his gift to the body of Christ. God's plan for mankind was one of blessing and purpose. Embracing Christ's redemption on the cross leads us back to our spiritual Eden, and in this book, Pastor Lee clearly shows us all the way.

—JIMMY WITCHER
Senior Pastor, Trinity Fellowship

FLOURISH

PLANTING YOUR LIFE WHERE GOD DESIGNED IT TO THRIVE

LEE M. CUMMINGS

DEDICATION

I am dedicating this book to two different people. The first is my grandparents, Roy and Joan Cummings, who raised me to love God, love God's Word and especially His Church. I was able to flourish as a young man in the call that God had upon my life because of the example of these wonderful lovers of Jesus. The second people I want to dedicate this to are the people of Radiant Church. It has been an incredible honor for Jane and me, to lead a congregation of people that truly love God with all of their heart, soul, mind and strength. Over the last twenty three years, we have seen Radiant grow from a seedling of an idea to a flourishing tree of life in the midst of our city and generation. Thank you Radiant, for following so passionately. The best is still yet to come!

FLOURISH by Lee Cummings
Published by Radiant City Media
8157 East DE Avenue
Richland, MI 49083
www.radiant.church

Unless otherwise noted, all Scripture quotations are taken from the Holy Bible, English Standard Version. Copyright © 2001 by Crossway Bibles, a division of Good News Publishers. Used by permission.

Scripture quotations marked KJV are from the King James Version of the Bible.

Scripture quotations marked NIV are taken from the Holy Bible, New International Version®, NIV®. Copyright © 1973, 1978, 1984, 2011 by Biblica, Inc.™ Used by permission of Zondervan. All rights reserved worldwide. www.zondervan.com. The "NIV" and "New International Version" are trademarks registered in the United States Patent and Trademark Office by Biblica, Inc.™

Scripture quotations marked NKJV are taken from the New King James Version®. Copyright © 1982 by Thomas Nelson. Used by permission. All rights reserved.

Scripture quotations marked NLT are from the Holy Bible, New Living Translation, copyright © 1996, 2004, 2007. Used by permission of Tyndale House Publishers, Inc., Wheaton, IL 60189. All rights reserved.

Scripture quotations marked THE MESSAGE are from *The Message: The Bible in Contemporary English*, copyright © 1993, 1994, 1995, 1996, 2000, 2001, 2002. Used by permission of NavPress Publishing Group.

Scripture quotations marked TPT are from The Passion Translation®. Copyright © 2017, 2018 by Passion & Fire Ministries, Inc. Used by permission. All rights reserved. ThePassionTranslation.com.

Visit the author's website at www.radiant.church

International Standard Book Number: 978-0-578-53587-6

While the author has made every effort to provide accurate internet addresses at the time of publication, neither the publisher nor the author assumes any responsibility for errors or for changes that occur after publication. Further, the publisher does not have any control over and does not assume any responsibility for author or third-party websites or their content.

19 20 21 22 23 — 987654321
Printed in the United States of America

CONTENTS

Foreword by Jimmy Evans. vii

Chapter One
   ENVIRONMENTAL ISSUES. 1

Chapter Two
   **BETHEL—THE REVELATION
   THAT CHANGES EVERYTHING**. 13

Chapter Three
   CREATED TO FLOURISH 34

Chapter Four
   REDEEMED TO FLOURISH. 55

Chapter Five
   ANOINTED TO FLOURISH 69

Chapter Six
   FLOURISH IN YOUR IDENTITY 90

Chapter Seven
   FLOURISH IN COMMUNITY. 104

Chapter Eight
   FLOURISH IN YOUR DESTINY 116

Chapter Nine
   FLOURISH IN YOUR PROCESS. 134

Chapter Ten
   FLOURISH IN YOUR LEGACY 148

Notes 156

FOREWORD

The story of God and His people begins in a garden. The first chapter of Genesis takes a lofty, almost poetic approach to Creation, but the first real *place* in Scripture is the Garden of Eden.

None of us have ever lived in a perfect paradise like Adam and Eve, but we can relate to a garden. I grew up in Amarillo, Texas—a windswept city in the middle of the flat Panhandle, where we were lucky to get twenty inches of rain a year—and I still don't have any problem imagining a lush, green garden. It's a compelling image.

There's nothing more captivating to humans than a flourishing garden that's been tended well by an expert gardener.

Is that why God created the Garden of Eden for the first man and woman?

Is humanity's innate attraction to green spaces related to that history?

I believe so.

In the Bible, gardens aren't limited to the Creation story. Jesus was in the Garden of Gethsemane when He agonized with God before His arrest and crucifixion. Surrounded by His friends, He chose this serene setting prior to taking on the sins of mankind.

After the crucifixion, John 19:41 says Jesus was buried in a tomb in a garden. In the next chapter, Mary Magdalene saw the risen Christ and even mistook Him for a gardener.

Besides these significant moments, consider how often Jesus spoke about seeds, planted fields, vineyards, and branches. Agriculture dominated life in first-century Israel, so obviously those themes appeared all the time in His parables.

But there's also an incredible connection between the story of Jesus and the symbolism of a garden. In your backyard garden and in the Garden of Gethsemane, life springs up from death. A tiny acorn can become a mighty oak. A single, planted kernel can turn into an ear of corn. In just a few carefully cultivated generations, that one kernel can create an entire field that feeds thousands.

There's something special about gardens, and that's one reason I believe God named the first garden Eden. In the ancient Hebrew, the name *eden* means "pleasure" or "delight."

God gave Eden to Adam and Eve to give them pleasure.

God placed the first humans in a garden to delight them.

God created us, like the plants in a lush, properly tilled garden, to thrive.

I've known Lee M. Cummings for many years. We've collaborated on projects together, and I'm honored to be an overseer of Lee's church. I've visited Michigan, where Lee lives and serves, and let me tell you—it's a much greener place than where I grew up. Michigan is a place where developers cut down trees to make room for houses and streets. Where I grew up, developers *plant* trees to beautify a new neighborhood, because green things don't grow there naturally. Compared to the tumbleweeds and yucca of my childhood, Kalamazoo is practically the Garden of Eden.

That said, we both see the beauty in living things. I believe Lee, in this book, has a truly valuable message about the importance of our spiritual environment and where we plant our lives. He is absolutely correct when he writes that we were created to thrive and designed to be fruitful. It's written into our DNA, and that supernatural design is a reason we are so attracted to peaceful green spaces.

We were created for gardens. We were created to flourish.

As Lee reminds us, Psalm 92 says the righteous "are planted in the house of the Lord and flourish in the courts of our God." I'm praying for you as you read the chapters that follow. May you have open eyes to see the beauty He's given us, and an open heart that allows the Master Gardener to plant you where you'll flourish—today, tomorrow, and for the rest of eternity.

—JIMMY EVANS
Senior Pastor, Gateway Church
Southlake, Texas

Chapter One
ENVIRONMENTAL ISSUES

God is an environmentalist. If that statement shocks you, let me draw the picture I want you to see with a little more detail.

An environmentalist is someone who believes that the quality of our natural surroundings—air, soil, and water—have a defining effect upon our long-term health and development. Along these same lines, someone can take their passion for the environment and formalize their interest by studying environmental science and becoming an environmental scientist. If we look closely at God's Word, we will discover that God cares about the environment also—our environment—and instructs us to maintain the right one for our spiritual health. In this way, God is an environmentalist.

The difference between God and an environmental scientist is the scientist can only observe the effects and attempt to identify the cause or causes. God, on the other hand, is the Creator of everything in the natural and supernatural (or spiritual) arena. Therefore, He is certain of the long-term effects because He Himself is Lord over all. He is the uncaused Cause.

This is not to say everything that happens is the result of God directly causing it to happen. We understand that one of the outcomes of God's creating man with free-will agency is a world that became subject to man's will rather than the perfect will of God. There is often a conflict between God's will and man's determination. This is a result of the fall of mankind in the garden, a subject we will come back to further on in this book. The garden was a perfect environment that God created for His image bearers. The problem of sin was born there, not in the soil but in the soul of Adam and Eve, throwing the rest of creation into a tailspin of death, decay, and the full ramifications of rebellion.

Yes, God is the cause or the Creator of mankind. Some would say that means He is the Creator or the cause of all that has gone wrong with the world. This conundrum of the cause of evil has been contemplated for millennia by the best minds among us and still remains difficult to understand. What is abundantly clear is, even though God may not directly cause all things, He is directly redeeming all things. In fact, God is bringing these things together to serve His purpose, and His purpose is that these things would work for our good and to His glory in the end.

> For I am God, and there is no other; I am God, and there is none like me, declaring the end from the beginning and from ancient times things not yet done, saying "My counsel shall stand, and I will accomplish all my purpose."
> —ISAIAH 46:9–10

If you have ever wondered if God cares about the difficult and painful places you have found yourself in during some of the hardest times of your life, the answer is a resounding yes! He cares more than you know. He not only sees, but He is also passionately on your side to bring you through the battles and into the wide-open places of victory and peace. There is no devil in hell, no offense of another, or no mistake you could make that would cause God to stop loving you or keep Him from reworking your current situation into something new. Part of God's glorious plan of making all things new and restoring our lives has to do with environments.

There is a lot of controversy in our day about climate change and what part of the impact is man-made and how much of it is cyclical. In August 2018, the United States was hit by two Category 4 hurricanes. Hurricanes Florence and Michael ravaged the coastlines of Florida and the Carolinas. Then a third storm threatened those same coasts until it was steered away and finally dissipated. We have also been experiencing some of the warmest temperatures on record in Michigan, while other parts of the country are experiencing colder than normal temps.

What is causing all of this? Is it just the natural course of our weather to change and shift on its own, or have man's industrial endeavors combined with a massive multiplication of population begun to take a toll on environmental conditions?

Among the talk in our day, some discussions revolve around how vital the environment is and the call for people to become more aware of how the changing environment affects not only us today but also how it will impact future generations.

Our understanding of spiritual environments is also a critical issue for Christians and the church as a whole to understand. What we don't know can impact us now and our children and their children for years to come. Having eyes to see and ears to hear what the Spirit is saying can lead us into a revelation that will set the stage for what God wants for us today, tomorrow, and on into the future.

While I am neither qualified nor courageous enough to take on the issues of natural climate change in this discussion, I do want to speak very boldly about the significance of a healthy spiritual environment and the impact it has on the development and maturity of every follower of Jesus. That environment is the church, the house of God.

Flourishing in the House of God

Psalm 92 is a foundational psalm revealing to us how God sees the church as a spiritually rich environment, perfectly formed for His people to thrive in. Verses 12–15 tell us that:

> "the righteous shall flourish like a palm tree, he shall grow like a cedar in Lebanon. Those who are planted in the house of the Lord shall flourish in the courts of our God. They shall still bear fruit in old age; they shall be fresh and flourishing, to declare that the Lord is upright; He is my rock, and there is no unrighteousness in Him" (NKJV).

Notice that the righteous are compared to trees that find the right soil. This is how God sees us in relationship to His house. Trees are used throughout Scripture to describe God's people as rooted, strong, and fruitful.

I happen to love trees. I am fascinated by them, really. I love to walk through the forests near our home and look at the different species and the various ages of each tree. There is something majestic about tall, old trees. When I look at them, I wonder how old they are and the things that they have witnessed over the years, the storms they have endured. When I see one that is decaying and dying, I often wonder what caused the life of something so solid and flourishing to come to an end. Most of the time, it is the environmental conditions that cause it to thrive or die.

In the life of a son or daughter of God, there is nothing more important than the spiritual soil in which we are planted. Like a tree, we draw nutrients from that soil by anchoring our root system deep into our surroundings. The health of the soil determines the health of the tree. Soil that is deficient of key nutrients spells disaster for the tree. Literally, the soil determines the level of growth potential the tree will be able to realize over the course of time.

Whatever environment a Christian chooses to plant their lives in will determine the level at which they are able to fulfill their purpose, because not all soil is equal. It may look the same on the surface, but there are certain spiritual nutrients only present in the place that the Bible describes as "the house of the Lord."

In the same way that not all soils are equal, regardless of what they look like on the surface, not everything that calls itself the "house of the Lord" is an environment that promotes spiritual flourishing. It's a simple thing to place the word *church* over the door of a building, but that doesn't automatically make it an environment conducive to thriving in spiritual health. It has far more to do with the elements of the Spirit than the structures shaped by man. The house of God is different than the dwellings of men. The church that Jesus is building is a house of revelation and presence. It is a house in which the Father is very much at home in the midst of His family. There is order in this house—and honor. When these characteristics are present, a heavenly environment is established on the earth. It's like Jacob's ladder being dropped down from the heavens, touching the earth, giving access between heaven and earth.

Like a Flourishing Palm Tree

Consider a rare species of palm tree known as the chandelier tree, or its more scientific name, *Pandanus candelabrum*,[1] a species that grows primarily in tropical West Africa. Recently it has been discovered that this particular kind of tree seems to thrive primarily in areas where there are subterranean kimberlite and lamproite pipes formed by ancient volcanic eruptions under the surface. These volcanic pipes are known to be rich in potassium, magnesium, phosphorus, and sodium, which form the perfect fertilizer mix for the chandelier tree.

What is even more fascinating about this new discovery is that, in addition to these volcanic pipes being rich in these certain minerals, they are also highly concentrated containers of diamonds that have been pushed up toward the earth's surface from their deep reserve. This new information stands to change the way the diamond industry and diamond hunters go about looking for this precious, yet difficult to find, commodity. Now all they will have to do is fly over vast miles of jungle wilderness and search for large clusters of these unique palm trees to know where to dig for diamonds.

I can't help but see the parallels between this game-changing discovery and what the Bible tells us about God's plan for His people to be planted in His house. There is something unique about the soil of the church that causes us to flourish. The local church may not always look like it's flourishing on the outside, but it has something deep within its reserves necessary for spiritual growth and maturity. If we miss it or overlook it, we will be in danger of living out our faith in less-than-favorable conditions and not seeing the full realization of our destiny in God.

In much the same way as geologists can now look at a healthy chandelier tree and know that there are costly and rare gems below the surface, the world should be able to look at the church and know that there is something rare and beautiful there, something that can only be found in its unique spiritual environment.

Rooted and Grounded

For a tree to grow healthy and strong, it not only needs soil with the right mineral composition, but it also needs a strong root system that gives it stability and will allow it to draw in the nutrients and water it needs. The soil can be packed with everything a tree needs, but if the roots cannot access what it needs, the tree will not flourish.

There is an organic process that takes place in which the roots go deep, searching for what the tree will need for life. The roots then draw in the water that carries the nutrients. This process also activates the genetic programming of the plant.

Every tree starts as a seed, which contains all of the genetic material and mapping for its entire lifespan. An acorn is a coding container for a mighty oak tree, but the process of growth will only be initiated once it is buried in the soil—planted. Once the seed finds the right soil, the plant begins to put out roots in order to draw in from the soil all of the life-giving ingredients it will need to grow. If the seed never finds the right soil, the potential within it will lie dormant until it dies. This is similarly true of the believer.

Paul the apostle wrote in Colossians 2:5–11:

> For though I am absent in the flesh, yet I am with you in spirit, rejoicing to see your good order and the steadfastness of your faith in Christ. As you therefore have received Christ Jesus the Lord, so walk in Him, rooted and built up in Him and established in the faith, as you have been taught, abounding in it with thanksgiving. Beware lest anyone cheat you through philosophy and empty deceit, according to the tradition of men, according to the basic principles of the world, and not according to Christ. For in Him dwells all the fullness of the Godhead bodily; and you are complete in Him, who is the head of all principalities and power. —NKJV

The strength of our faith is determined by our spiritual root system. We develop strong roots when we intentionally determine to put our lives in the place where the Spirit of God is at work and where we get connected to the source of our life, the Lord Jesus Christ. Conversely, if we don't cease drinking from the streams of culture and drawing from the soil of this world's philosophies, we may start off believing in Christ and have all the right intentions but soon find ourselves depleted, barely surviving instead of spiritually thriving. We become the product of whatever spiritual soil we are rooted in. If it is the world, we won't grow spiritually strong in Christ to live out our full potential and end up cheating ourselves of a heavenly inheritance.

Making Jesus Christ the Lord of our lives is the single most significant decision we can make. Deciding to get planted and rooted in the house of God, the local church, is the next most pivotal decision because it determines whether we grow strong and become built up into mature sons and daughters of God, or whether we will become stunted in our growth, shrivel up, and die altogether.

As a healthy tree is the result of being planted in the right soil, so is a flourishing child of God. It was never God's intention to save us and then leave us vulnerable and fruitless. God's design and desire is for every believer to tap into the spiritually vital soil of the local church, draw living waters from the subterranean rivers of God's Spirit, and live fruitful lives full of impact, joy, and peace.

When our root systems are healthy, our lives will be healthy. When we are grounded and unoffendable, our future will be undefeated. We were created new in Christ Jesus to silence storms with heaven's peace, eclipse the darkness with the light of God's glory, and demonstrate the superiority of heaven's culture over the broken lies of a fallen society that promises the world but delivers only hell on Earth. In short, you were called and created to flourish.

What would it look like if we grew in such a way that we endured the storms of life? What would it look like if our root systems were so deep, and we were planted in the optimal place where God's process of maturity could take happen? Is it possible to live out our faith in such a way that, when the rest of the world is tired and worn out, we are still bearing fruit? Are there vital elements about the house of God that aren't naturally apparent to us but are necessary for the purposes of heaven to be borne out through us? Has God in His manifold wisdom designed and crafted spiritual environments that feed our soul and nourish His purposes from seed to root and from shoot to fruit?

I believe with my whole heart that the answer to these questions is yes! God has given us a promise in these verses that we can and will flourish when we are planted in God's house. If we want to live out the world's genetic code of death and disappointment, all we have to do is feed off the natural, basic principles of living. The Book of Proverbs tells us that there is a way that seems right to a man (the world's way of living) but the end leads to death (14:12).

But if we are going to grow up in God and become mature sons and daughters, demonstrating the full manifestation of our kingdom genetic traits, we are going to need to get rooted in Christ and be planted in His house.

Your Spiritual DNA

Every tree grows to the exact specifications of the DNA it carries. Only in the last few decades have we become aware of how intricate the genetic mapping of everything is. Trees, for example, start as seeds, but their future, size, shape, and fruitfulness are already coded within them, waiting to be fleshed out when they reach their mature states. Every human being, upon conception, also receives a nature and set of chromosomes from their parents that determines everything about them: eye color, height, and hair thickness or baldness. Even the physical mannerisms we will display are determined.

As a child of God, the Bible is clear that we become "newly created" and receive a new spiritual nature when we are born again, into the family of God:

> ...by which have been given to us exceedingly great and precious promises, that through these you may be partakers of the divine nature, having escaped the corruption that is in the world through lust.
>
> —2 PETER 1:4, NKJV

In essence, when we are born again, spiritually speaking, we receive a brand-new genetic code, which is imprinted on our spirits. This spiritual DNA contains the immutable promises from God concerning who we will be when we grow up in Christ and what God intends to do through us (fruitfulness). First Peter 1:23 puts it like this:

> ...having been born again not of corruptible seed but incorruptible through the word of God which lives and abides forever.

With the Holy Spirit dwelling within us, we receive an impartation of the "divine nature" of Christ as the prototype for our regeneration. He has the genetic code to which we are to be conformed. Literally, the full potential of God's eternal purpose for us is deposited in our spirits waiting to be unleashed. It is just waiting for the process to begin and for the environmental factors to be aligned.

But just like a natural seed, the genetic code will not begin to process until it is buried below the surface of the right soil. The environment is just as much a factor in seeing the fullness of the tree's potential lived out as the seed itself. If all you have is soil, you have an opportunity. If all you have is a seed, you have potential. If the two are ever brought together, you will see the full lifespan and fruitfulness manifested for all to see.

There are so many Christians who are carrying around their new nature in Christ in its seed form. They are frustrated because they sense that there is something great inside them, but they don't know how to make what's hidden become visible. They've been living their lives from day to day, not seeing the change and transformation they thought would happen. They can't put their finger on it. They just know that they were created for so much more.

Have you ever been in this place? The enemy subtly lies to you by insinuating that there's some deficiency or something wrong with you. Doubt takes over, and you begin to question whether you are even saved. Perhaps he's made you feel as though there was something defective in your conversion experience. But what we are here to discover is that the underlying reason for these issues has more to do with whether or not you have made a deliberate decision to be planted in the church, the house of God. It's not so much that you aren't growing or in progress; it's that your growth process has been slowed and hindered by what you're missing. You aren't flourishing because you haven't realized the importance of putting your roots down into the right spiritual soil and allowing the life that flows from the kingdom of God to activate the maturing process and thereby bring about the full and fruitful life you were created for.

Potted Not Planted

All right. I can hear you saying, "I go to church every weekend. How is it that still feel that I am missing something?"

OK, let me start here: church attendance in our culture is an interesting conversation. The statistical information over the last two or three decades indicates that people are attending church less and less regularly. Fifty years ago, the vast majority of the American population identified themselves as Christians (whether the label was accurately applied is a whole different discussion we're not going into at this time). Church attendance on Sundays was normal, the rest of society, as a whole, shut down on Sundays because it was somewhat of a sacred day of rest, worship, and family focus. It seemed as if everyone went to church, even if they weren't devout or even Christian.

Today, nothing could be further from the truth. Fewer and fewer people identify as "Christians," and even among those who do, church and church attendance are viewed as good but optional. Culture as a whole has seized hold of the opportunity to do other things on Sundays. What used to be a day that everyone took a step back has become filled with sport activities, patronizing businesses, and even work as if it were a Thursday. Church has ceased to be a priority as it once was.

I believe there are direct correlations between the lack of priority for gathering as the church on Sundays and the breakdown of our effectiveness Monday through Saturday. The lack of priority of Sunday morning church attendance shows up in the decline of the nuclear family and even the the moral convictions of the Christian community as a whole. Not that church attendance alone changes anything, but in the case of individual Christians' attempting to live out their faith in the midst of a very dark world, is it possible that a default decision to neglect the life-giving environment of the house of the Lord has left us more shaped by the compromising ways of the world? Are we being swept downstream by the strong currents of culture without even knowing it is happening? This is exactly what will happen if we don't quickly reconnect with how significant our gathering together as a church is to our spiritual health. Attending church is more than an option.

However, only attending services is not the cure-all either. Merely entering a building and giving a cursory listen will not produce the kind of flourishing God desires for each of His children. It's about more than going, sitting, kneeling, and praying. It's about *how* we are approaching the invisible attributes of church that matter most. If church is a building only in our estimation, we will never go deeper in our understanding or commitment. The tool that tills up the soil of church and give us access to plant our roots down deep in this spiritually rich environment is an obedient response to this revelation that the church has more to it than meets the eye. When we respond with awe, wonder, and dedication, our lives become planted and positioned to take root.

Think about a garden whose soil is made up of beautiful, rich volcanic matter that has all been tilled and made ready to receive the roots of a young, potted palm tree. The caretaker brings the five to six-foot-tall palm, held in a temporary plastic pot, and plops it down onto the ground. The roots of the palm are bound up in a small ball inside the container, just centimeters away from the soil that would feed it, anchor it, and cause the young sapling to expand, grow, and reach its massive potential. But the caretaker never takes the plant out of the pot. He just leaves it on the surface! Can you imagine? Because of this, the tree never grows any larger. Its potential becomes stunted, and it could even become root bound and die.

This is the story for many Christians. They are "in the church," but they have never allowed their lives to be truly planted in the house of God. They are potted but not planted. They may be standing right next to another believer who is thriving, growing, and steadfast in their faith, and in the natural, there is no distinction between the two. The difference has to do with what is unseen, below the surface.

One is rooted and drawing from the anointing that is present and gives stability and nutrients for growth. The other is unstable and is easily blown over by the storms of life. One is growing tall in their faith and bearing fruit; the other wants to and is trying to become better on their own but hasn't realized that the environment around them is what activates the destiny within.

If this resonates with you, I want to encourage you that God has so much more for you. In His house are the true riches of His inheritance for you found in the company of the saints. In His house is everything you need to fulfill His purpose for your life and the peace and power that cannot be found anywhere else. Mingled within the soil of the church is every spiritual mineral that has ever been depleted by a world gone wrong. These minerals are ready to give life to your soul and elevate you above the limitations of sin's gravitational pull. It's all there waiting for you to tap into.

In this book, we're going to dig deep below a surface understanding of the local church and gain insight into the spiritual terrain. All the favor you've ever wanted and all the provision you will ever need are available to you. The protection of a loving Father and the power of His Holy Spirit are ready to be unleashed upon your life.

If God is an environmentalist, then we should be too. If it matters to Him, it should matter to us. The Bible exhorts us, "It is the glory of God to conceal things, but the glory of kings to search things out" (Proverbs 25:2). We're going to discover what it looks like to flourish in our understanding, our calling, and our identity as children of God, destined to thrive in

God's presence. With this spirit, I invite you to come with me to the next chapter where we are going to focus on receiving the same revelation that shifted everything for the biblical patriarch Jacob.

I believe with all of my heart that this revelation is a game changer and has the potential to change the trajectory of your life. If we will respond in the same way that Jacob did, the promise that we find in Psalm 92—living a flourishing life in the courts of God—will become a reality and the days of living short of our full potential will be left behind.

Chapter Two
BETHEL—THE REVELATION THAT CHANGES EVERYTHING

Jacob was a young man on the run. He had left behind everything he knew to pursue something he wasn't sure existed—satisfaction for the longing he felt in the deepest part of him. An uncanny descriptor of who he was and how he had gotten to this point in life, the name *Jacob* means "supplanter," "deceitful,"[1] or in my words, "sneaky." He didn't choose this name, but his actions throughout his life solidified this notorious label and became the very reason he became a man with burnt bridges and no place to call home. When you read the details of Jacob's life in the pages of Genesis, you notice that, from the beginning, personal ambition and an inner need to be loved and accepted drove him to do things that got him in serious trouble with his family, especially his brother, Esau.

Every family has its unique dynamics, but growing up in Isaac's home left Jacob empty and envious. Jacob was a momma's boy in the truest sense of the word. His older twin brother, Esau, was dad's favorite.

Esau was a man's man—strong and aggressive—a real take-charge type of guy, who pleased his father over and over with the wild game his hunting trips produced. But while Esau was winning acceptance and favor with his father, Jacob was left on the sidelines hungering for the position and things that had eluded him. If we read between the lines a bit, we can see a young man who spent much of his life feeling left out in the cold, literally, from his father's tent of affection and preference. So it shouldn't be surprising that Jacob did what many of us do in similar situations: he took matters into his own hands. He conspired with his mother, Rebekah, to devise a scheme that would turn over to him the favor and blessing he desired.

Having observed Esau's daily routine, Jacob was able to catch Esau in a vulnerable moment of hunger and tricked his brother out of his birthright.

> Once when Jacob was cooking stew, Esau came in from the field, and he was exhausted. And Esau said to Jacob, "Let me eat

some of that red stew, for I am exhausted!" (Therefore his name was called Edom.) Jacob said, "Sell me your birthright now." Esau said, "I am about to die; of what use is a birthright to me?" Jacob said, "Swear to me now." So he swore to him and sold his birthright to Jacob. Then Jacob gave Esau bread and lentil stew, and he ate and drank and rose and went his way. Thus Esau despised his birthright.

—GENESIS 25:29–34

Jacob may not have been as burly as his older brother, but he was smart, outwitting him and convincing him to give away his most valuable possession. In Genesis 27, we see where Jacob was clever enough (and desperate enough) to convince his father, Isaac, to release Isaac's supernatural, generational blessing upon himself instead of Esau. Jacob pulled this heist off by covering his arm with an animal skin in order to replicate his brother's apparently very hairy arm. I'm not quite sure how hairy you have to be for the hair on your arm to be compared to animal fur, but it must've been significant, to say the least.

Lying under the shadow of his tent, the aged Isaac, drawing close to death with his sight deteriorating, fell for his son's scheme and laid his hands upon him, imparting the blessing that originated in his father Abraham's covenant with God Almighty. Jacob finally had laid hold of what he always wanted, or so he thought.

As you can imagine, once the conspiracy was made public to his brother and father, he became *persona non grata* and quickly realized that his reach for blessing had left him running for his life. His actions made things so bad that, at the prompting of his mother, he gathered his things and ran before the fury of his scorned brother could catch up to him.

The Place the Ladder Dropped

Based on how the Scriptures describe Jacob, I imagine that this departure from his home and family started in his heart years earlier. Jacob had lived his whole life striving to carve out a place of significance in his family. His body had been present, but his heart and mind were always on a search for a sense of identity and significance. After tricking his brother out of his birthright, Jacob's journey took on a tangible reality as he tried to find a place to sleep for the night on his way to Paddan-aram. There wasn't a family connection or home, which would offer Jacob hospitality, or he would've accepted. For this searching son, there was only wilderness and wasteland. The name *Luz* actually means, "to turn aside." It can also mean "place of refuge when turned away."[2]

Both of these meanings fit where Jacob was at this moment in his life. He had turned away from the path of integrity, choosing instead to become a self-made man. Now he had been turned away by his own family. He had no other choice but to take a rock for his pillow and make the rough ground his place of rest for the night. While Jacob sought to find sleep in this land of in-between, God broke into his fear-filled mind and imagination with a dream, giving Jacob a divine revelation of Himself that would change everything.

> Then he dreamed, and behold, a ladder was set up on the earth, and its top reached to heaven; and there the angels of God were ascending and descending on it.
> And behold, the Lord stood above it and said: "I am the Lord God of Abraham your father and the God of Isaac; the land on which you lie I will give to you and your descendants. Also your descendants shall be as the dust of the earth; you shall spread abroad to the west and the east, to the north and the south; and in you and in your seed all the families of the earth shall be blessed. Behold, I am with you and will keep you wherever you go, and will bring you back to this land; for I will not leave you until I have done what I have spoken to you."
> —Genesis 28:12–15, nkjv

Jacob awoke with such an awareness of God's presence that it stunned him. Here he was in the middle of nowhere, feeling as lonely as he ever had, and yet now, he understood that the place he thought was empty and void in the natural was filled and alive with truth. All he could offer in response was, "Surely the Lord is in this place, and I did not know it" (v. 16, NKJV). What Jacob said next encapsulates the entirety of the encounter.

As Jacob gathered himself after this divine encounter, I imagine him trying to process the gravity of the display of glory he'd just witnessed and how it left him both afraid and protected at the same time. He was in awe when he said, "This is none other than the house of God, and this is the gate of heaven" (v. 17, NKJV).

In the midst of his extreme loneliness and rejection, self-loathing and wandering, he had found a home within the presence of God—a place of acceptance despite his shortcomings. For him, it was more than an encounter of the supernatural kind. Jacob had intersected with the heart and purposes of the God of his father and grandfather. In a moment, his perspective of who God was and who he was himself was altered.

The House of God

There is so much significance to the imagery in Jacob's vision. The key to it all is the concept of a house, and not just any house, but the house of God or, as Jacob named it, *Bethel*. If you think about it, many of us relate a house to a place where a family dwells together. Even if our own experience is not ideal, we ourselves have a longing for what we know a family and a house are *supposed* to be. It is where children are loved and raised and taught to know who they are and to honor those who have gone before them.

The house has a table where each of the family members come together and sit at the place appointed for them. It's where the family name describes those who live within its walls, shaping a sense of identity and belonging. A household is where the resources and wealth are managed and distributed with those precious heirlooms, which are handed down as an inheritance, being kept and handled with care. No one goes into the house unless invited, and no one leaves without being noticed.

Every household has a head. The father or mother of the household gives leadership and nurture, serving as a gatekeeper of sorts. If you want someone to stay over, you don't ask the siblings or the neighbors; you ask the head of the house, whoever that may be.

In Jacob's case, God had established the house that he was being invited into. The door had been opened, and standing at the door was the God of Abraham, Isaac, and now, Jacob. It was none other than the house of God. In that house, Jacob was no longer standing on the outside looking in, even though there were no physical walls. The walls of fear and unsurety had been demolished by a single breakthrough moment from the heavenly

Father, and he now found himself standing right in the middle of the living room—an awesome place to be!

Many of us can identify with Jacob's personality and painful past. I am so glad God didn't only choose *ideal* people to be the main characters in His redemption story but instead chose the flawed and weak, the overlooked and underestimated. And like them, many of us know what it is like to live without an *ideal* family or any family at all. So many have silently suffered with dysfunctional mind-sets left over from their pasts and have struggled to see how the future could ever be different. So when we see Jacob's painful struggle to find his place, we can identify with it.

There is something in each of us that drives and motivates us to search for meaning and a place to belong. Family and home are supposed to instill that, but often they don't, leaving us to search for it in other places. We try to define ourselves, make a name, prove our worth, and prove to people that we are worth loving, but rarely do we find that place of security on our own. We play these games with God also, attempting to get His attention, gain His approval, and garner His favor and grace. We make deals with God, run from Him when we know we have failed, and yell at Him for what appears to be His lack of fairness or concern.

A vision like what Jacob received is exactly what we all need in the midst of our journey. We may not literally traverse no-man's land, but we know what it's like to be turned away or to live with the repercussions of our own burned bridges. The irony of modern society is that there are more people on the planet than ever before, yet there are more of us who are feeling disconnected, lonely, and lost.

Is there a place where we belong? Is there something we are missing? I believe Jacob's dream is not only a message from heaven for him but also for us in our day. We already know God promised to bless Jacob and that the blessing he would receive would in turn bless all the families of the earth. Could it be that part of that blessing is this revelation of the house of God? Could it be a truth-filled blueprint for all of God's people, in every age? I believe it is.

The Prophetic Promise

It's important to understand *why* a revelation is so important in shaping our response to God. A revelation is far different than mere information. Information only communicates details or facts. If information alone had the ability to change our perspectives, the world would be a drastically different place, and increasingly so, since we have more information at our disposal than any other generation before us. We would be quickly moving toward utopia.

I recently read an article that said mankind is creating more information every two days than we did from the dawn of civilization until the year 2003. The amount of information that the average person has access to instantly is shocking to consider. Our smartphones have more computing ability than the computers that put man on the moon! We are living in a day when there is such a massive acceleration of information and technology, yet we are still struggling with the same issues that we have since the beginning. Information doesn't change people's lives; revelation does.

> Where there is no vision [no revelation of God and His word],
> the people are unrestrained.
> —PROVERBS 29:18, AMP

Revelation is different than information alone. Revelation has a divine element attached to it that breaks through our previous awareness and brings us into a new realm of understanding. It removes the barriers of ignorance. Like a seed, it contains within it the germ form of change and alteration. Instead of seeing information from our own biases, revelation comes with heavenly bias. When Jacob awoke from his dream, he realized that he had just encountered Almighty God. With that revelation came more than a new hope. He had a sudden realization that he was not left alone to chart his own path, as he had previously believed. We see the light bulb turn on for Jacob, when he makes this statement:

> If God will be with me and keep me in this way that I go, and
> will give me bread to eat and clothing to wear, so that I come

again to my father's house in peace, then the Lord shall be my
God. . . .

Genesis 28:20–21

He was putting to words what he had come to understand about the
revelation God had shown him. The information was in the details of the
vision. The revelation was in the takeaway of what it meant for his future.
God gives us revelations as scale models of our prophetic future. We don't
necessarily have all of the details, but faith arises within our spirit when
we are convinced of God's future and plan for how He will get us there.
Ultimately, this plan serves to redeem what has been lost and brings us
into His destiny for our lives.

Jacob's Response

I have heard it said that life is 10 percent what happens to us and 90 percent how we react. I believe there is a lot of truth in that statement. Jesus
said that we would know the truth and the truth would set us free (John
8:32). The only truth that has the capability of bringing freedom and
change to our lives is the truth that comes through revelation knowledge.
There is tremendous change that can occur once we have gained heavenly
insight through the Holy Spirit who leads and guides us into all truth. But
it requires action on our part.

If Jacob had not responded in faith to the revelation he had received,
his story would've looked much different in the end. But what we find in
his response is humility, awe, and child-like faith. His response opens for
us a prophetic invitation. We see not only the promise of God, but the
faith-filled response of man that bore out the fruit of destiny. It becomes
clear that God's design and intention for the church is to become a spiritual greenhouse, in which regardless of the environment or season that is
transpiring around us in the world, we can confidently be planted and
flourishing. This is what we find in Jacob's story from this point on, and
it's what God wants to be true about your story from this point on as well.
It has everything to do with what you will do with this revelation. If you
embrace it and let it get rooted in your spirit, you are heading toward an
ambush of God's divine favor upon your life. If we ignore it or reject it, we
will continue to live as orphans, continually on the search.

There are three important actions Jacob took in response to what He learned about God:

1. Setting the stone
2. Pouring the oil
3. Testing the tithe

Let's take a deeper look at each of these now.

The Setting of His Stone

In Genesis 28:18, the Bible tells us that "early in the morning Jacob took the stone that he had put under his head and set it up for a pillar." This was Jacob's first response after receiving his life-changing revelation: take the stone that had served as his pillow the night before and set it up as a pillar.

In ancient Near East culture, setting up a pillar carried tremendous meaning. A pillar was used functionally as a support system to hold up the roof or structure of a building. On a more specific level, it meant establishing a place of worship or a temple. Jacob's awakening to the reality that God was with him and revealing Himself to him in this place led Jacob to commit himself to this location as a place where he would worship God for the rest of his life. In other words, Jacob's setting up of the stone is a picture of making a commitment to building and supporting the house of God.

Unfortunately, the word *commitment* has become a negative or derogatory word in American culture. We know it's an important word and principle, but one we don't want to apply. We are the culture that is connected to everything but committed to little. The attack on commitment is epidemic in every arena of our lives. A prime example of this is the divorce rates. Fifty percent of marriages will end in divorce. Unfortunately, this statistic is almost the same within the marriages of those identifying themselves as Christians (although recent data indicates that the divorce rate is significantly lower among self-identifying Christians that attend church regularly).[3] The idea of "until death do us part" has been replaced by "until I no longer feel the same about you as I do now."

Loyalty in the marketplace also reflects this. A generation ago, people would work for the same company for thirty years and then retire with the security of a pension. Today, many companies are cutting retirement benefits and forcing older employees into early retirement in order to hire younger replacements for future wages. These companies are also moving jobs overseas where labor is cheaper, thus bolstering the bottom line, something now viewed as "corporate responsibility" to their respective shareholders. On the other side of the paycheck, many younger people, new to the workforce, are changing jobs every few years, bored and in search of gaining a variety of experiences before "settling down."[4] The lack of commitment from one party has led to the lack of loyalty on the other. It has produced an impersonal marketplace environment in which high level commitment is rare.

Part of this is due to our lack of understanding of what commitment looks like and how sacred our power of decision really is.

Don't fall into a "second-wallet" mentality.

All of the membership cards we have to things to which we aren't really committed is a great example of this. Think about it. How many discount cards, coffee shop punch cards, and membership cards do you have? I actually have a second wallet in which I keep all of my membership cards to things I rarely use. I leave my second wallet in the consul of my vehicle to pull out on those rare occasions when I may patronize one of these locations where I am a supposed member.

If I am going in to the popular vitamin/supplement store in the mall, I hopefully remember I have the Gold Card membership that entitles me to ten percent off. Or if I stop by the local coffee roaster to buy a bag of Ethiopian beans, I pull out my punch card so I can eventually get a free bag after ten bags purchased. Other than that, the cards stay in their place. My commitment to these places is based upon a convenience or service. At one time, there may have been a sense of excitement upon discovering such a place, but after a while, the newness or necessity of it waned.

If you were to ask me about the organizations or causes of which I am a committed part, these establishments wouldn't even enter my mind. I would mention family, church, and charitable groups that I partner with around the world to improve people's lives. These are the things that I live for and to which I have a significant commitment. You won't find them in my second wallet.

In our Western way of living, a belief in God is almost expected. A majority of Americans would even define themselves as "Christian" (although that number is slipping dramatically). But if you were to ask many of those same people how significant their commitment is to a church community or environment, you might be surprised to see how many people have placed the house of the Lord into their second wallet. Church might get pulled out, so to speak, at Christmas, Easter, or other special occasions, but it hasn't become a vital part of our understanding of what it means to truly flourish in life.

The Mystery of Membership

Setting the pillar of our heart's commitment, like Jacob did, is a massive step in spiritual development for positioning ourselves to flourish in God's purpose for our lives. Having a second-wallet mentality is embracing the attitude of a consumer, where you begin to see the house of God from the outside looking in. It leads you to think such things as, "I will keep the house of God close in mind, in case I need something or want something from it."

A consumer is far different from a contributor. Consumerism sees the church as a product to take or leave, but the true meaning of membership is connectedness. The apostle Paul used very specific language to describe the church as a body with many *connected* members.

> For as in one body we have many members, and the members do not all have the same function, so we, though many, are one body in Christ, and individually members of one another.
> —ROMANS 12:4–5

Understanding our spiritual connectedness to one another amplifies the need for our commitment. We aren't spiritual prosthetics, interchangeable and disposable. The living flow of the Spirit of God circulates through our interconnected and interdependent vascular system originating in the heart of God. Our movement and purpose are intertwined with one another, and when one part is not functioning or is damaged, it affects the rest of the body. The revelation of the body of Christ, as received by the apostle Paul, is a great and beautiful mystery that can only be understood through the eyes of the Spirit.

> This mystery is profound, and I am saying that it refers to Christ and the church.
> —EPHESIANS 5:32

There is incredible power and beauty within the principle of commitment. The way God views relationships and commitment is the polar opposite of how this world views such things. The way the world ensures we keep our commitments is through legal contracts. God's way of expressing His commitment toward us is through a loving covenant. From the Garden of Eden all the way through the age to come, God is revealed as a covenant-keeping God.

A contract culture is developed in the darkness of mistrust and fear, always preparing us for the worst-case scenario. Our culture and society are sick with fear and starving for the bedrock of unconditional love and commitment to build our lives upon. How we, as the children of God, demonstrate the countercultural commitment to the Lord and one another is one of the most potent prophetic signposts we can erect. I believe when the world sees the covenant relationships Christians have within the church, it will attract and provoke those in the world who are searching for something to belong to and to give their total devotion.

If we only replicate the same consumerist attitude towards the house of the Lord that is already apparent in the world, we will not attract the lost and searching. But if we can tap into our spiritual genetic code as spiritual children of Abraham, we can demonstrate to the world a new level of what covenant relationships look like. The church is poised to no longer follow the pattern of this world's broken commitments and mistrust, but we are poised to elevate the culture of covenantal faithfulness that provokes a generation of Jacobs in search of a sense of belonging and family.

Pouring the Oil

The second significant response of Jacob to the Bethel revelation was to pour his oil out over the stone pillar he set up as a pillar representing his commitment.

So early in the morning Jacob took the stone that he had put under his head and set it up for a pillar and poured oil on the top of it.

—GENESIS 28:18

All throughout the Scriptures, oil is symbolic of the anointing of the Holy Spirit, as well as the gifting and empowerment of an individual as given to them by God. The term is related to the verb "to anoint, to smear."[5] When a priest or a king was ordained, they were anointed with oil, representing the supernatural empowerment of God being laid upon them for the office or calling they were to fulfill.

The word or title *Christ* comes from the Greek transliteration of the word for "the anointed one." The literal meaning of the word *anointing* comes from the Greek word *Christós*, literally "the Anointed One," a translation of Hebrew *Messiah*. Jesus referred to this at the beginning of His ministry in Luke 4 when He read from the prophet Isaiah:

"And he came to Nazareth, where he had been brought up. And as was his custom, he went to the synagogue on the Sabbath day, and he stood up to read. And the scroll of the prophet Isaiah was given to him. He unrolled the scroll and found the place where it was written,

"The Spirit of the LORD is upon me, because he has anointed me to proclaim good news to the poor. He has sent me to proclaim liberty to the captives and recovery of sight to the blind, to set at liberty those who are oppressed, to proclaim the year of the Lord's favor."

And he rolled up the scroll and gave it back to the attendant and sat down. And the eyes of all in the synagogue were fixed on him. And he began to say to them, "Today this scripture has been fulfilled in your hearing."

—LUKE 4:16–21

Oil represents the anointing of God personified in the Messiah, or the anointed one, which then flows by God's grace as a deposit in every child of God. There are no ungifted people in the body of Christ because everyone who belongs to Jesus has the Holy Spirit dwelling inside them. God has rubbed off onto each of us something of the anointing of Jesus, because each of us are a part of His body. This means that each believer also is equipped with spiritual giftings, which are manifestations of the Spirit's anointing within. Consider the following scriptures:

> But the anointing that you received from him abides in you, and you have no need that anyone should teach you. But as his anointing teaches you about everything, and is true, and is no lie—just as it has taught you, abide in him.
>
> —1 JOHN 2:27

> Having gifts that differ according to the grace given to us, let us use them: if prophecy, in proportion to our faith; if service, in our serving; the one who teaches, in his teaching; the one who exhorts, in his exhortation; the one who contributes, in generosity; the one who leads, with zeal; the one who does acts of mercy, with cheerfulness.
>
> —ROMANS 12:6–8

> Now there are varieties of gifts, but the same Spirit; and there are varieties of service, but the same Lord; and there are varieties of activities, but it is the same God who empowers them all in everyone. To each is given the manifestation of the Spirit for the common good.
>
> —1 CORINTHIANS 12:4–7

> But grace was given to each one of us according to the measure of Christ's gift.
>
> —EPHESIANS 4:7

There is an oil reservoir inside you. It is an anointing that is present because the Holy Spirit of the Anointed One dwells in you. Where will you direct the anointing that lies within you? Will it be poured in the place of covenantal relationships, forging unity, or will it indiscriminately be poured out in empty, barren places? Jacob poured his oil over the top of the pillar that he set. As we recall, the pillar represents the place of his rest, the house of God. To pour our oil upon *our* pillar is to intentionally direct our giftings and affections first and foremost to the building of God's house.

We have been entrusted to faithfully steward the oil of anointing deposited within us. God expects us not to ignore the gifts and callings given to us but to invest them in the things He is doing on the earth. The primary thing God is doing is building His church one living stone at a time, calling us to join Him in what He is building. This is why Paul refers to us as co-laborers with God (1 Corinthians 3:9). God enjoys inviting us into His purposes, to work alongside Him. First, we have to come to grips with the fact that regardless of what we have thought about ourselves or what lies we have believed, we are anointed and called for "good works":

> For we are His workmanship, created in Christ Jesus for good works, which God prepared beforehand, that we should walk in them.
>
> —EPHESIANS 2:10

Once we have embraced the truth that we have the oil of heaven within us, we must then decide what we are going to use it for. So many people recognize that the gifts and grace upon their lives are God-given, yet they use them for their own pleasure or agenda. This is the equivalent of randomly pouring oil out on the soil outside. It will only be soaked up, leaving little trace of its presence. It is the same when we use our gifts to fulfill our own agendas; they are soaked up by temporal satisfaction or acclaim. While there is nothing wrong with maximizing our talents for career purposes or helping others, the highest purpose of every gift or anointing in a believer is for kingdom purposes.

If we only see the church as secondary in importance, we will continue to look for and find our significance in other avenues and fail to invest the oil of our lives in the one environment God created specifically for us to flourish. The church has become stigmatized as a place where we donate our leftovers and give our spare time. What would happen if we saw the church the way heaven sees it? What if we prioritized our time, talent, and resources appropriately?

Think about the way Eugene Peterson translates Paul's statement about the church from Ephesians 1:

> At the center of all this, Christ rules the church. The church, you see, is not peripheral to the world; the world is peripheral to

the church. The church is Christ's body, in which he speaks and acts, by which he fills everything with his presence.

—vv. 22–23, The Message

Commitment may be a dirty word to the world, but it is a foundational pillar within the kingdom that not only gives support to what God is building on the earth but also gives each of God's children a place to belong and develop a God-centered identity.

You weren't made just to go to church, but you were created to be a significant part of the church, a living stone set in its prepared place and thriving. A church is not just an ethereal idea, but it is a living community, in a geographical location, where you set your stone and begin to pour out your oil in sacred service to advance the kingdom of God.

The Test of the Tithe

Jacob's third and final response to the revelation of the house of God had to do with his wealth. It was a vow that he made to God that was measurable, definable, and sacrificial. It was attached to the promise over his life that God would prosper him and bless him and fulfill the destiny upon his life.

"And of all that you give me I will give a full tenth to you."

—Genesis 28:22

The biblical concept of giving God a tenth is called *the tithe*. The concept of the tithe was nothing new to Jacob; it ran in his family. In Genesis 14, we read about his grandfather, Abraham, who had received the call and the promises from the Lord. Abraham had also offered God Almighty a tithe as an act of worship and a declaration of covenantal devotion. When Abraham and Lot had settled in the land of promise, they decided to separate from one another and live in different areas. Upon separating, Lot found himself kidnapped by foreign armies. He and his servants, flocks and family were taken captive, and their lives were endangered. Once Abraham heard this, he and a handful of his servants pursued these massive armies in order to get Lot back. Against insurmountable odds, Abraham and his ragtag team of servants defeated these armies, and not only got his family back, but they also recovered wealth beyond what was lost.

Upon returning to the land, he was met by two mysterious figures. One was the king of Sodom, and the other was named Melchizedek, king of Salem, meaning *"king of peace."*[6]

The king of Sodom, a picture of the devil (Sodom always carries a sinful connotation in the Bible), requested to be given the *people* whom Abraham had rescued and told him to keep the wealth he had recovered for himself (Genesis 14:21). But then came Melchizedek, who brought bread and wine to Abraham and blessed him (Genesis 14:18).

> "Blessed be Abram by God Most High, Possessor of heaven and earth; and blessed be God Most High, who has delivered your enemies into your hand! *And Abram gave him a tenth (tithe) of everything."*
>
> —GENESIS 14:19–20, EMPHASIS ADDED

Most scholars acknowledge that Melchizedek represents at least a strong type of Jesus Christ. Some have conjectured that this may even be an Old Testament appearance of the Son of God, sometimes called a *Christophany.* The Book of Hebrews showcases Melchizedek as a divine parallel that resembles the Son of God. Even though it is doubtful that this is indeed Jesus literally, it definitely speaks to the priesthood role that Jesus operates in as our eternal Mediator.

I find it interesting and significant that the king of Sodom tempted Abraham to sin against God by encouraging him to keep his wealth for himself and surrender the people over to him to do as he wished. This temptation is as contemporary as it is ancient. Satan always tempts God's people to see money and wealth through a self-serving lens. What we often overlook is that, when we fail to honor God with our finances, there are eternal ramifications affecting people, meaning there will be people who are not reached, rescued, or brought into the Promised Land.

We see Abraham giving a tenth of everything he had gained to this king and priest. He overcame the tempting offer from the king of Sodom and instead honored God by giving a tithe to this king who is a type of Christ. In doing so, he recognizes his divine blessing is from God above and his future prosperity will be the result of God's favor and not his own hands.

For this Melchizedek, king of Salem, priest of the Most High God, who met Abraham returning from the slaughter of the kings and blessed him, to whom also Abraham gave a tenth part of all, first being translated "king of righteousness," and then also king of Salem, meaning "king of peace," without father, without mother, without genealogy, having neither beginning of days nor end of life, but made like the Son of God, remains a priest continually.

—Hebrews 7:1–3, NKJV

Now Jacob, a couple generations later, awoke from this dream and, as I imagine, recalled the stories he had heard his grandfather share about how the Lord had originally spoken to him. He must have recalled this story in particular of how God had supernaturally guided Abraham into the land of promise and preserved his life and wealth in the face of threats, enemies, and lack of a permanent home to call his own. As he was contemplating how to seal his vow before God, he made this commitment to recognize God as his protector and provider from that day forward by offering a tenth of all he had.

The principle of the tithe is found throughout the entirety of the Bible. Giving God the first tenth of our financial increase as a declaration of our covenant dependence on Him is a powerful test of our loyalty and a reaffirmation of who we've accepted as our true source.

One of the purposes of tithing has to do with our hearts. When we put God first with our finances, the tithe serves as the tithe serves as an antidote to the love of money and greed. Jesus said it is impossible for us to serve God and money.

No servant can serve two masters, for either he will hate the one and love the other, or he will be devoted to the one and despise the other. You cannot serve God and money.

—Luke 16:13

In similar fashion, the apostle Paul indicates that one of the greatest threats to the soul of a believer is the *love* of money. The subtle diseases of greed and selfishness are like cancers to the human spirit and can cause us to swerve in our devotion to Jesus.

> For the love of money is a root of all kinds of evils. It is through this craving that some have wandered away from the faith and pierced themselves with many pangs.
>
> —1 TIMOTHY 6:10

The other important purpose behind the principle of the tithe is that it is used to finance the gospel. It takes money to build the church and preach the gospel. While obviously God could miraculously provide finances from heaven if He so desired, He chooses to partner with His people. It is a divine test of our wills moved by faith and also a beautiful partnership between heaven and Earth, as we give materially to what God is building spiritually in the earth.

The central theme of the Book of Malachi is to call God's people to return to the Lord. In their minds, Israel had never left God. They continued to go through the motions of religious life, but in their hearts, they had ceased to depend upon the Lord and keep Him at the center of their focus. God had taken a back seat to their own pursuits and desires. It is within this context that God raised up the prophet Malachi with a series of questions to ask. One of the questions was, "Will man rob God?" Their response to that question was, "How have we robbed you?" (Malachi 3:7–9).

It is interesting that, when God began to call them to return their devotion to Him, the first thing the Lord points out is that they have ceased giving their tithes and offerings. God's solution for their returning to a place where their hearts were healthy and devoted began with their restoring the practice of tithing. Why? Because of the tether between the heart of man and the love of money. Jesus spoke of this connection at length when he said, "For where your treasure is, there your heart will be also" (Matthew 6:21).

Money (along with politics, sex, and race issues) is one of the most challenging subjects to talk about in church. Nothing makes people squirm more and listen less than when the topic turns to money. This should be a tip off to us that there is something else going on under the surface. Beyond our field of vision, spiritual warfare is waging. Do we believe everything we have belongs to us or to God? Do we really believe God will keep His word and supernaturally provide for us, or will we allow our heart to subtly be seduced by fear and selfishness?

Sam Houston, one of the founders of the fourth largest city in the US, was once asked why he was so generous with the church. It is reported that Sam gave a significant amount of money to build the first church in the beginning city of Houston, which is named after him. He even single-handedly paid the necessary financial support so that the congregants could have a full-time minister instead of an itinerant preacher. His answer to the question of why he did this is quite telling. He said, "When I got baptized, so did my wallet!"

What an answer. He understood something many others miss. If we want a healthy community, we need a healthy church. Sam had a healthy revelation of the house of God.

The Book of Malachi is the last book in the Old Testament, where God calls to His people to return to Him completely. God said that the first step in returning to Him was returning the first tenth to Him. In other words, the first thing we can do to demonstrate the return of our hearts to their first love is to stop robbing Him and once again honor Him. When we take the miraculous provision of God over our lives for granted, it leads us to subconsciously believe that we are somehow capable of taking care of ourselves. We miss the miracle and rob God of the honor He deserves and the opportunity to bring greater blessing into our lives.

The place God had always designated as the place for His people to bring the tithe is His house. In the Old Testament, His house was the tabernacle in the wilderness or the temple of Solomon. This is where the storehouse of provision was maintained under the auspices of the priests.

> Bring the full tithe into the storehouse, that there may be food in my house.
> —MALACHI 3:10

In the New Testament, the house of God is no longer a physical temple, but instead it is a spiritual temple made of *living stones* called the church. It is also referred to as the household of faith. (See Galatians 6:10.) Worship and honor aren't issues of geography per se, but cardiology. Giving is always an issue of the heart.

There is a difference between living under the economy of self-sufficiency that has been cursed since the fall in the garden and living under the covenantal blessings of God's economy. The tithe is a spiritual key of recognition that gives us access to the blessing of open heavens over our lives and finances. Whether it is portrayed as a ladder or open windows, the concept is the same.

It's easy to see from God's perspective that the dual purpose for the tithe is to provide spiritual food in His house and also protect us from self-dependency. In a very practical way, this means that, when we give the tithe of our increase, not only are our hearts realigned with God's covenant promises, reminding ourselves that God is our provider, but we are also helping set the spiritual table for those who are hungry and thirsty for God to come and feast.

As it turns out, however, less than 10 percent of evangelical Bible-believing Christians in the US actually honor God with a tenth of their finances even though the American church is by far the wealthiest group of Christians on the planet.[7] Third-World Christians display greater generosity in many cases, even though they have far less material wealth. I am not sure of the reasons why money is such an issue for those who have so much, but I do believe it is a demonic strategy birthed in hell to keep the church stagnant and lethargic in our mission to reach the world.

I believe with all my heart that, if we had a healthy revelation of the church and our role in it, giving would be our response to the faithfulness of God. If we understood more fully God's faithfulness and commitment to our destinies, the act of pouring out our oil and honoring God with the first fruits of our increase would be an overflow of our faith and thankfulness.

Just as Abraham received a prophetic revelation of God's covenant faithfulness through the bread and the wine, and Jacob was assured of the promise of restoration of all that he had lost, we also can receive a revelation of God's purpose for His house. Maybe we too need a revelation that causes us to see God's house—the church—differently.

The house of God is not just an institution for us to frequent on holidays; it is an icon of God's presence in the midst of a lost and dying world. It is a colony of heaven and a greenhouse of destiny, where those planted in its rich soil grow to maturity by drawing upon the heavenly nutrients. And the more they are fed and nourished, the more they display the values and vision that are written upon the spiritual genetic code of the children of God.

There is so much more to the house of God than meets the eye. The church contains an awesome atmosphere that is charged with the supernatural potential of the kingdom of God. It provides a staircase of exchange that allows us to access all that is necessary from heaven to equip and empower us to fulfill our purposes here on Earth. It is a household, where God the Father sits at the head of the table and looks at each one of us and calls us by name—the name by which only He knows us.

The house of God is all of this and more, but we must receive a new set of eyes to see all it encompasses. We need the kind of eyes that only revelation granted by the Holy Spirit can open. If God will do it for a young deceived and broken young man named Jacob, then I believe He will do it for us as well.

Chapter Three
CREATED TO FLOURISH

Every four years, I look forward to the Summer Olympic Games. My wife, Jane, and I enjoy watching all of the track and field events, as I relive my high school days of being a pretty decent athlete. It's amazing how easy it is to get caught up in the pageantry and patriotism of watching the US athletes compete in their events, even in sports that we know very little about.

One of my all-time favorite athletes to watch is Michael Phelps. Michael holds the Olympic record for the most medals won as well as several world and Olympic records for various swimming feats. Watching him prepare for a race and finally explode into the pool at the split-second sound of the starting gun is a marvelous thing to witness. He's won eight gold medals at the 2008 Olympic Games in Beijing and a total of twenty-three Olympic gold medals. I believe it's safe to say that Michael Phelps was made to swim.[1]

That's not just a kind way to describe someone who has been successful in their chosen field. Experts say that a big part of what makes Michael Phelps so fast in the water, beyond his incredible drive and work ethic, is the way his body is designed.

Standing at six feet, four inches and 194 pounds, Michael also boasts a six-foot-seven-inch wing span. His torso is much longer than that of someone his height, with legs that are proportionally shorter. His size 14 feet serve as powerful flippers, and the ankles that hold them are able to hyper extend further than a trained ballet dancer, giving them the ability to powerfully thrust his feet through the water. When evaluated, specialists have come to one conclusion: Michael Phelps was made to swim. And swim he does.

Created for More

There is nothing more exhilarating than watching someone discover what they were created to do. An artist or athlete, a woman becoming a mother for the first time, or a young man strumming a guitar—it's as if a light goes on and something deep inside them awakens, something they didn't know was even there. Now that they know it, they can never *un*know it. They will forever be different, changed, and more fully alive than they have ever been.

Human beings were created to flourish from the very beginning. God created a good world, and mankind was His crowning creative achievement, designed and destined to thrive. Most people live ignorant to this truth. When we look at the human condition today and the societies that we have built, all we can see is the devastation and death that plagues this planet. Too many times, we ask the difficult questions of life such as "If God is so good, why does He allow such bad things to happen?" or "Why did God make the world so cruel?" We are making certain assumptions that things, as they are now, are the way they were always meant to be.

God's original intent and purpose for humans was drastically different than our present reality. He didn't create us to fail, falter, or live in fear. He created us to flourish in every facet of life as His sons and daughters. Deep down inside the human heart we know that there is something wrong with the way things are. This awareness should be an indicator that there is a right way for things to be. It's as if the inner person inside each of us is longing for what it knows has been lost. Life disconnected from God is like looking at a broken mirror lying on the floor. We can see our own reflection in the broken pieces, but it's marred and splintered. Putting the pieces back together is an arduous and daunting prospect that keeps most at a stalemate. How do all the pieces go back together? What if I get it wrong? What if I injure myself in the process? Most just accept that the brokenness in their lives and the lives of those in the world around them is just the way it is, instead of searching for a solution. Others do attempt to put the pieces back together by setting out on a self-help journey, only to burn out from discouragement and the realization that we don't have it within ourselves to heal ourselves.

An inner turmoil remains, which leads to a continual sense of angst, because we know that we were created for more and better. We want to be whole and healthy and to experience the peace that comes from having our lives in proper alignment. We long to live a life of purpose and meaning.

We want meaningful relationships, not just shallow intersects. We hunger for a connection with our Creator, but we don't know which road to take.

The way to move forward into the flourishing life begins with going back to the beginning to decipher the original design that God had in mind for His good creation. If we can find what we have lost, it will point us forward into what needs to be restored.

Fruitful by Design

In the opening chapters of the Book of Genesis, we see that the first way God reveals Himself to us is as Creator. Genesis 1:1 says that, in the beginning, God created. He set the stage by creating the universe—the stars, sun, and moon—and then moved closer as He placed His focus on Earth. Speaking the mountains and oceans into their places, He filled them with beautiful and exotic animals. He decorated the skies with clouds and the ground with a variety of vegetation. When it was just the way the Lord God wanted it, He began His masterpiece—man.

The Bible tells us that, when God created humans, He didn't just speak us into existence; He made us with His own two hands, shaping and crafting us like a master artist working the clay.

> Then the Lord God formed the man of dust from the ground and breathed into his nostrils the breath of life, and the man became a living creature.
>
> —Genesis 2:7

Adam was different from all of the rest of the creatures that the Lord God had made. Everything else served as the backdrop on the stage to the central actor in God's drama. Man was made differently because God's design and destiny for man was distinct from all of the rest of creation. God expressed His design, desire, and destiny when initiating the creation of man.

> Then God said, "Let us make man in our image, after our likeness. And let them have dominion over the fish of the sea and over the birds of the heavens and over the livestock and over all the earth and over every creeping thing that creeps on the earth." So God created man in his own image, in the image of

God he created him; male and female he created them. And
God blessed them. And God said to them, "Be fruitful and multiply and fill the earth and subdue it, and have dominion over
the fish of the sea and over the birds of the heavens and over
every living thing that moves on the earth."

—GENESIS 1:26–28

There is special significance in going back to the first mention of things
in the Bible. When something is introduced for the first time, you find its
origin as well as its purpose. Here, we find the first mention of humanity
and the explicit purpose that God had in creating us. It's important to
know that mankind was not random, unexpected, or an evolving overflow of other created things. We stand apart from everything else in the
economy of God because of the purpose for which we were created. This
is vital, because if we don't see how special we are as the centerpiece of all
that God created, we will be susceptible to the lie that we have no unique
purpose and are mere spin-offs of other species. In fact, God had four very
specific purposes in creating us: identity, dominion, family, and destiny.
Let's briefly look at each one.

Purpose #1: Identity—reflecting God's image

God's primary purpose for creating mankind was to bear His image to
the rest of creation. When God said, "Let us make man in our image, after
our likeness" (v. 26), He did not say this to imply that God Himself is a
man. In fact, the opposite is true. Man was originally created to reflect the
Divine. When God spoke the words, "in our image and likeness," He said
this to indicate *how* man was created. Like God, humans are crafted to
be self-aware of their own being and, thus, to contemplate the meaning of
themselves and everything around them. Created as creative beings, there
is an innate understanding that our first order of existence is to seek after
meaningful purpose. God is a God of order, purpose, and reason. When
God created Adam, and by extension all human beings proceeding from
him, he was equipped with this same desire and ability to bring order to
chaos and live from reason and not random instincts.

Though God had the angels at His beck and call, as they are servants of
His will, He still desired something more. Created as His sons and daughters, humans were intended to represent God to the rest of His creation.

37

Even the very way God crafted humans to be three-part beings of body, soul, and spirit is ever-present evidence of the triune Godhead of Father, Son, and Holy Spirit.

> Now may the God of peace himself sanctify you completely, and may your whole spirit and soul and body be kept blameless at the coming of our Lord Jesus Christ.
>
> —1 Thessalonians 5:23

The word *represent* means to be a constant reminder of not only the existence of a creator out there somewhere beyond their ability to behold, but of the nature and nearness of God. Even the word itself carries deep revelation. To *re-present* God means to repeatedly present or put forth the image and attributes of God that reflect back to creation as a constant reminder.

When man entered an environment, it was as if God Himself had stepped in. Man walked in complete authority that was born out of his intimate connectedness to Father God. He was the walking and breathing expression of the will of God. Another way of describing how Adam bore the image of God is to see him as the icon of God. An icon is an image that represents an idea or a person. Most of us have icons on our computers that represent a program or operating system. When we click on it, we know to what we are gaining access. This is what it means to bear the image and likeness of God as His representative. We represent God's wisdom, plan, and authority. We were created to be like Him.

The idea of the *imago dei*, or "image of God," and its significance can be found in the prohibition of other images. In the Ten Commandments, we see God forbids the crafting and worshipping of graven images.

> You shall not make for yourself a carved image, or any likeness of anything that is in the heaven above, or that is in the earth beneath, or that is in the water under the earth. You shall not bow down to them or serve them, For I the Lord your God am a jealous God.
>
> —Exodus 20:4–5

Idolatry was and always has been one of the greatest traps and tactics of the enemy. The temptation to reshape God into the image of our own liking is an act of spiritual treason. The fall of man has produced an inverted reality of our making God into our own image so He can represent our will in heaven as it is on Earth instead of how it was originally designed to be: us carved out of the earth and made in God's image and likeness in order to represent His will and purpose on Earth as it is in heaven.

Purpose #2: Dominion—exercising heavenly authority

The second thing that the Bible tells us about man, connected to God's purpose, is that God gave him dominion over the earth and the things that dwell in it.

> And let them have dominion over the fish of the sea and over the birds of the heavens and over the livestock and over all the earth and over every creeping thing that creeps on the earth.
> —GENESIS 1:26

In God's original design, mankind had been delegated authority from heaven over the entirety of the world. Everything belonged to Adam and was under his direct influence. Man was God's co-regent over all of the rest of creation. He was not on equal footing with the animals; he was charged with the responsibility of bringing government and order over the entire earth. In a sense, God had deputized Adam as the king or regent of the earth. If we look closely at the text, we realize it was not just an authority to manage what already was, but there was also an authority to finish what God had started in the garden, which we will discuss more in just a little bit.

In verse 28 this delegation is expanded upon when it says, "Be fruitful and multiply and fill the earth and *subdue it*, and have dominion over…" (emphasis added). The Hebrew word for *subdue* literally means "to tread upon or create a path; to bring under subjection."[2]

This means that life outside the garden potentially had some level of disorder and chaos. We obviously know that Satan, the deceiver, was present at creation, that he later took the form of a serpent, and that he followed the process along, positioning himself to turn God's creative intentions upside down for his own purposes.

Regardless of his schemes, it was by this command that Adam and Eve were delegated the responsibility to extend the boundaries of God's beautiful garden to the rest of the world, and ultimately to dominate the devil and his legions of demons. Instead, they forfeited this delegated authority to the deceiver by falling for his temptations (see Genesis 3), thus turning over the keys given to them by God Himself. Perhaps this is why millennia later, when Satan tempted Jesus in the wilderness, Satan said to Jesus, "To you I will give all this authority and their glory, for it has been delivered to me, and I give it to whom I will. If you, then, will worship me, it will all be yours" (Luke 4:6–7).

It was never God's design for mankind to be under slavery or servitude. Man was created to reign with God in a partnership with God, uniting heaven and Earth. This authority lost was later won back and restored by Jesus through His victory at the cross and vindicating resurrection. Paradise lost has now been reconstituted in the people of God and the dominion mandate is still in place.

> "All authority in heaven and earth has been given to me. Go therefore and make disciples of all nations, baptizing them in the name of the Father, of the Son and of the Holy Spirit."
> —MATTHEW 28:18–19

Purpose #3: Family—fruitfulness and fullness

The third facet of God's purpose for mankind has to do with family. Family is the center of God's plan for everything. When God first formed Adam, there was awareness on the Father's part that there was something lacking. The need for connection, intimacy, and companionship could not be met by any of the other creatures He had made. The only aspect of His created order that God declared was *not good* was Adam's aloneness.

> Then the Lord God said, "It is not good that the man should be alone: I will make him a helper fit for him."
> —GENESIS 2:18

God knew that Adam needed a suitable companion, so He fashioned one who would meet Adam's physical and emotional needs. Then He went further and designed it so that out of their love and intimacy, multiplication of the human race would take place. Man and woman, in loving union, are intrinsically gifted to create new life, another facet of the image of God. Even though God is the Author of all life, He has given His co-regents the gift of determination. We choose when to have a child, and how many we will have in most cases.

Our culture often sees children and the responsibilities that come with them as inconveniences or distractions from real living. It is said that we need to do all the things we want to do before we have kids because ou best years are the years before we are strapped down with kids. The abortion industry in our society is terminating hundreds of thousands of lives every year on the altar of convenience. From the beginning, the devil has been on an all-out assault against children. He knows God desires nothing more than to see the earth filled with godly families and filled with children growing in the security and knowledge of God and His Word.

Parents who walk in a new-creation reality will raise children who love God, love His Word, and will grow up to love the house of God and fulfill their destinies.

> Did he not make them one with a portion of the Spirit in their union? And what was the one God seeking? Godly offspring.
> —MALACHI 2:15

It's interesting that the first institution God brought into being was family. Family serves as the foundation of God's global plan and the basis for belonging and transmission of purpose. The roles of a family reflect our relationship with God and the relationship within the Godhead, again revealing aspects of the image of God to the rest of God's world.

Purpose #4: Destiny—divine partnership

It was never God's plan to create the heavens and the earth, stand Adam up in the garden, and then exit, leaving it all in Adam's hands. There are some, called deists, who do believe that God is in fact our absent Creator. They believe in the idea that the universe is a great cosmic clock, that God formed and wound up, just to let go and watch it unwind. This caricature of a cruel and emotionally detached deity is not the true picture of the Creator we read about in the pages of Scripture.

We see very clearly that God, our all-powerful Creator, is not only transcendent, but He is also very intimate. He is the God who is over all but, equally important, the One who draws near into relationship with us. As we see the story of history beginning to unfurl in the beginning, we see the Lord God, concerned with the well-being of His co-regents and children. We find Him coming daily to walk and converse with Adam and Eve as a Father would.

> And they heard the sound of the LORD God walking in the garden in the cool of the day.
>
> —GENESIS 3:8

God's intention from the beginning was for He and Adam together to fill, fashion, and rule the earth as Father and son. Literally, this responsibility was meant to be a family business. Together, they were to craft the world into a temple for the glory of God to fill with His Presence. The garden served as a scale model for Adam to work from as he moved out into the new unchartered territories of Earth with the authority and presence of God upon him as he replicated God's beauty and design. Then, as Adam and Eve would have children and their children would have children, their family would expand and fill the earth with the godly seed. The knowledge of the Lord would cover the earth like the waters covered the seas. This project of building the earth into God's sanctuary would require a partnership of trust and obedience. God would intimately instruct Adam in the truth, and Adam would reflect God's truth to the rest of creation and embody the wisdom of the Father, expanding the boundaries of God's will and reign.

The Garden of God

If you've grown up in church, the story of creation and of Adam and Eve in the Garden of Eden is a foundational story. I don't know about you, but when I picture this scene, I immediately go back to flannel-graph boards and coloring sheets that were passed out to us in our Sunday School classes. In my imagination, I picture a lush, green botanical garden, a few acres in size, with a couple standing naked in the middle of it all, surrounded by trees and vines.

We don't know much about what the Garden of Eden really looked like, but we do know from Scripture some of the descriptions and dynamics that made it special. The first thing that we know is that God planted it.

The garden didn't just appear; it was specifically designed as an environment man could flourish in.

> And the Lord God planted a garden in Eden, in the east, and
> there he put the man whom he had formed.
>
> —Genesis 2:8

The Hebrew word for *garden* is *gan*, which is better translated, "a place of protection, shelter and guardianship."[3] Yes, it was a beautiful place, but the thing that made it most beautiful was not the vegetation but the safety and presence of the Lord. The word *Eden* means "place of delight." Adam and Eve would live under the supernatural favor and blessing of God, and experience the delight and joy of life in God as long as they lived in this environment, where the primary boundaries weren't only geographical but also spiritual.

A garden can also be described as "a cultivated place." This is where our modern word *culture* is derived. The garden was a place prepared and established with the culture of heaven as its foundation. God, the Gardener, not only cultivated it with lush trees and fruitfulness, but He also created an environment rooted in love, order, and trust. As long as Adam and Eve trusted the Father, they would continue to flourish in unending life and shalom. Everything in the garden was good and complete, bringing joy and delight, the way God intended it to be.

Part of how God crafted mankind was to give them the gift of volition or choice. Many have asked, "Why would God make man with free will knowing they would rebel and fall?"

The answer to that question lies in the sovereign wisdom only God possesses. What is obvious is this: in order for God to have the loving relationship with His children He desired, giving them the power to choose was a risk He would have to take. But, even in this, it is important to know God has never been mistaken or taken by surprise. He stands over everything, orchestrating the events of history in such a way that, in the end, His majestic wisdom and ability to bring all things together will be displayed and made evident.

God gave Adam everything, but He also gave Him boundaries for flourishing in this gift of life.

And out of the ground the Lord God made to spring up every tree that is pleasant to the sight and good for food. The tree of life was in the midst of the garden, and the tree of the knowledge of good and evil....
The Lord God took the man and put him in the garden of Eden to work it and keep it. And the Lord God commanded the man, saying, "You may surely eat of every tree of the garden, but of the tree of the knowledge of good and evil you shall not eat, for in the day that you eat of it you shall surely die."

—GENESIS 2:9; 15–17

Human beings were never meant to experience death, disease, failure, or loneliness. God created us to be regal sons and daughters, living in the fullness of life, sourced in intimacy and partnership with God and one another. Success in life wasn't something Adam and Eve had to strive for. It was the byproduct of living in divine relationship with God and His created order in obedience.

The destruction, pain, and broken cultures are the result of our own internal brokenness, not God's desired design. Just as much as Father God had an eternal purpose and blueprint for our flourishing, the devil had a diabolical strategy to disrupt God's plan, destroy what He created, and steal from Him the thing He desired most—a family of priests and kings.

Deceived

The garden was a perfect environment, not because its borders were impenetrable, but because the protection of the Lord surrounded man and woman as long as they maintained their devotion to Him and His instruction. Their obedience guaranteed that everything would function in perfect shalom (peace) and order. God didn't give them a list of legalities to keep. Instead, He gave them complete creative liberty over everything, except one tree (Genesis 2:17). This tree would become the test of obedience and trust. The instructions regarding which trees were good for food came to Adam and Eve even as they walked in constant and intimate relationship with God, stewarding creation as representatives of heaven. Their own relationship with one another was strong.Everything was as it should have been until the devil entered the scene.

Taking on the form of a serpent, Genesis describes the devil in his serpentine disguise as "more crafty than any other beast of the field that the Lord God had made" (Genesis 3:1). More than a mere snake, he took on this deceptive appearance as a fallen angelic being, because he was hell-bent on stealing for himself what belonged to God and that which had been entrusted to man.

Satan's deception against man in the Old Testament

The Old Testament doesn't give us as many answers about the devil or Satan as our need-to-know minds would like, but it does give us some clues into how this angel fell and how he now works against God's people. We see him at work in the heavenly courts of God accusing Job (Job 1:6) and instigating David to take a census (1 Chronicles 21:1).

Just as he stealthily entered the garden, he seems to be slithering his way throughout the pages of history, working in the shadows to keep humanity bound in sin and deception.

In Ezekiel 28, we find one of the passages that many scholars believe is more than just a prophetic oracle against an evil human king. It is believed that these verses have a dual prophetic meaning and point a finger at Satan's origin as well as his fall from heaven. Though the prophecy is addressed to the king of Tyre, there are some descriptions given in graphic detail that could not apply to a mere human being.

> Moreover the word of the Lord came to me, saying, "Son of man, take up a lamentation for the king of Tyre, and say to him, 'Thus says the Lord God: "you were the seal of perfection, full of wisdom and perfect in beauty. You were in Eden, the garden of God; every precious stone was your covering: The sardius, topaz, and diamond, beryl, onyx, and jasper, sapphire, turquoise, and emerald with gold. The workmanship of your timbrels and pipes was prepared for you on the day you were created. You were the anointed cherub who covers; I established you; you were on the holy mountain of God; you walked back and forth in the midst of fiery stones. You were perfect in your ways from the day you were created, till iniquity was found in you. By the abundance of your trading you became filled with violence within, and you sinned; therefore I cast you as a profane thing

out of the mountain of God; and I destroyed you, O covering cherub, from the midst of the fiery stones."

—EZEKIEL 28:11–16, NKJV

There is no way a mere man could've been in the Garden of Eden or had access to the mountain or presence of God. When we read that this being was covered in beautiful, precious gems, we see a creature that, in its original created form, would have reflected the glory of God with beautiful brilliance. This is an account of the creation and purpose of a being that God refers to as the "anointed cherub that covers" or "anointed guardian cherub." This is none other than Lucifer, or Satan, as he would come to be called. Originally, he was described as an angelic being, perhaps an archangel, who was granted closer proximity to the throne of God than any other creature.

If you've ever seen a replica of the Ark of the Covenant, you would have seen two golden cherubim hovering above the mercy seat, where the Shekinah glory or manifest presence of God resided. In Exodus 26, while on Mount Sinai, Moses received specific instructions on how to build the ark and the tabernacle. Is it possible that the design of the ark is based upon how God's eternal throne appeared to Moses on the mountain? The Bible doesn't tell us specifically, but if this is true, those two golden cherubim are physical depictions of the place Lucifer held in proximity to the throne of God before his eviction from heaven. Isaiah 14:12–15 tells us:

"How you are fallen from heaven O Lucifer, son of the morning! How you are cut down to the ground, you who weaken the nations! For you have said in your heart, "I will ascend into heaven, I will exalt my throne above the stars of God; I will also sit on the mount of the congregation on the farthest sides of the north; I will ascend above the heights of the clouds, I will be like the Most High." Yet you shall be brought down to Sheol, to the lowest depths of the Pit."

—NKJV

The bottom line is that pride and sin were found in Lucifer's heart, and he was expelled from the presence of God. This is oftentimes referred to as the "original rebellion" or "original sin." Isaiah prophetically recorded the confrontation in the heavenlies, when God evicted Lucifer. The Bible indicates that about one third of the angels joined Lucifer in this angelic rebellion against God and were also thrown out of heaven, becoming demons or evil, disembodied spirits (Revelation 12:4).

Satan's deception against man in the New Testament

In the New Testament, we learn more about Satan. We read in Matthew 4:1–11 that Satan tempted Jesus himself. There are also many instances where Jesus taught about Satan in detail, confronted him, and cast out demons. In Luke 9:18, Jesus stated that He saw Satan fall from heaven like lightning! This indicates that Jesus was present with the Father and the Holy Spirit when the original rebellion took place in heaven and that He was also responsible for casting Satan out.

Jesus wasn't the only New Testament writer to refer to Satan's fall. Paul refers to it in 1 Timothy when writing to Timothy about requirements for elders and leaders in the local church.

> He must not be a recent convert, or he may become puffed up with conceit and fall into the condemnation of the devil.
> —1 TIMOTHY 3:6

Jesus exposed Satan's true character and nature when confronting the corrupt ecclesiastical leaders of His day:

> You are of your father the devil, and your will is to do your father's desires. He was a murderer from the beginning, and does not stand in the truth, because there is no truth in him. When he lies, he speaks out of his own character for he is a liar and the father of lies.
> —JOHN 8:44

Peter warned fellow believers that the devil is a spiritual predator, constantly looking for the weak and vulnerable to pick off and that we must stay alert and vigilant:

> Be sober-minded, be watchful; your adversary the devil prowls around like a roaring lion, seeking someone to devour.
> —1 PETER 5:8

John the revelator describes to us the fall of Satan and his constant attacks and accusations against the saints of God throughout the whole world. These attacks and accusations are ultimately overcome by Jesus's victory on the Cross.

> And the great dragon was thrown down, that ancient serpent, who is called the devil and Satan, the deceiver of the whole world—he was thrown down to the earth, and his angels were thrown down with him. And I heard a loud voice in heaven, saying, "Now the salvation and the power and the kingdom of our God and the authority of his Christ have come, for the accuser of our brothers has been thrown down, who accuses them day and night before our God. And they have conquered him by the blood of the Lamb and by the word of their testimony, for they loved not their lives even unto death."
>
> —REVELATION 12:9–11

All of this helps us to gain an understanding of the devil's motives when he entered the Garden of Eden and deceived God's crowning achievement in creation—man.

Having lived in the presence of God for all of his life up until his prideful exit, he understood the perfection and beauty of being close to God. He understood the magnificent power that flowed from God's mouth with each powerful and creative word. I can imagine that Satan's hate and jealousy toward God only increased upon God's creation of man and woman. The intimacy that God cultivated with them and the anointing that He placed on their lives could have only reminded the devil what he had lost. Having experienced firsthand the angelic worship of God in heaven, he came to want that worship and adoration for himself. Why? The answer is pride.

Pride is the original sin found in Lucifer's heart. It is the sin that perverted his beauty, twisted his allegiance, and birthed the dream of a *coup d'état* against Almighty God. To think that he, a created being, could overthrow or even become an equal with the Creator of the universe is nothing short of insanity.

That firsthand knowledge filled Satan with such violence, anger, and drive to destroy everything that God had created. Like a shark drawn to the smell of blood, Satan and demons are drawn to attack the anointing because of whom it represents. Their single obsession is to overthrow and destroy it, and in doing so, remove the image of God from the earth. No other being in the universe understands better the implications of the anointing than Satan himself. He knows that, if there is anything that can destroy his efforts, it is the supernatural smearing of the power and glory of God upon His people. No one knew better than Satan the power of living in perfect unity under the shadow of God's favor and design with access to the throne room. I can only imagine how his hatred and anger boiled over as God bestowed these privileges upon mankind.

Deceived into Believing

To quench his seething emotions, the devil came at Eve with a lure and a lie. He appealed to her desires and baited her by portraying God as the deceiver instead of a trustworthy Father. The one tool in his playbook—to play upon man's pride—was one he knew well. It is the only contagion strong enough to destroy us from the inside out. As Eve gave ear to Satan's deception and lies, her attention was led away from the goodness of God and turned toward a sense of entitlement.

> Now the serpent was more cunning than any beast of the field which the Lord God had made. And he said to the woman, "Has God indeed said, 'You shall not eat of every tree of the garden'?"
> And the woman said to the serpent, "We may eat the fruit of the trees of the garden; but of the fruit of the tree which is in the midst of the garden, God has said, 'You shall not eat it, nor shall you touch it, lest you die.'"
> Then the serpent said to the woman, "You will not surely die. For God knows that in the day you eat of it your eyes will be opened, and you will be like God, knowing good and evil."
> —Genesis 3:1–5, NKJV

1. Discredit God's word

The first line of attack was to discredit the validity of God's word by calling it into question: "Did God actually say...?"

Then he led Eve to wonder, "Can God's word be trusted?"

This is the first instance of the devil utilizing what has become his weapon of choice. He knows the Bible better than any human being. He's been studying it for millennia, and he is a master at twisting it to say what he wants it to say—or better yet—what *we* want it to say. We see this in Matthew 4 during Jesus's forty days in the wilderness when Satan came to Jesus quoting the Bible at least three different times, trying to get Jesus to cave into His natural desires and to disobey His Father.

2. Portray God as less than loving

The second thing the devil did in his tempting of Eve was to portray God's motive as something less than loving. He made it sound as if God was holding out on her, because He didn't want her to reach her greatest potential. The devil made it sound like God was insecure in His relationship with her and Adam, and somehow had to keep them oppressed instead of liberated. He told her that they could be just like God if they wanted to, but only if they stepped out from behind the boundaries of God's commands and were willing to take matters into their own hands to eat the forbidden fruit.

You may have personally experienced the devil operating like this in your own life. He starts with challenging the truth that God has clearly spoken in His Word. Then he encourages us to be our own person and make our own decisions apart from God. He feeds the beasts of *self* and self-will, knowing that instead of our eyes becoming enlightened to our greatness, it will lead us to shame and separation.

3. Tell lies about identity

In the final movement of his masterful temptation, Satan lies to her about her identity. He says to her, "…and you will be like God, knowing good and evil" (Genesis 3:5). Why is this a lie? If we go back to the first chapter of Genesis, when God originally created mankind, He was explicit with the fact that we were already like God! He tricked her into thinking that she was somehow less than what God had made her to be. He stirred within her a lust for something that she already possessed.

When I read the words the serpent hissed, I hear him saying, "When are you going to live up to your potential? How long are you going to be a slave to this God? He's holding out on you. Come on. Live it up a little.

Chart your own course. You don't need Him or anyone else to tell you what to do."

The devil is a master at calling our true identity into question. He even did it to Jesus. Right after Jesus was baptized, anointed with the Holy Spirit, and received the public declaration from His Father that, "This is my beloved son, in whom I am well pleased" (Matthew 3:17), Satan came in with the challenge, *"If* you are the son of God..." (Matthew 4:3).

His tactics are no different today in dealing with God's sons and daughters. Even after we have been born again, filled with the Spirit, and adopted into the family of God, the devil still attempts to convince us that we are not accepted and not truly changed. Then he rolls archived video of our past, attempting to heap shame upon us and stir up the corpse of our old natures.

...Then Comes the Fall

The devil was successful at deceiving Eve and, by extension, Adam. Before we are too hard on them, let's remember that there isn't a single human being who hasn't also been tempted and fallen to the same game plan over and over. The only one who overcame Satan and never fell into his traps was our Lord and Savior, Jesus Christ, who was fully human yet sinless.

The results of Adam and Eve's failure were catastrophic. Immediately, they realized that they had erred and felt the weight of death encroaching around them and their souls, like a vine climbing up a wall, choking the life from them. They were naked, ashamed, and afraid of facing Father God. When He called out to them in the cool of the day, looking for fellowship, instead of running to Him, Adam and Eve ran and hid behind trees.

> And they heard the sound of the LORD God walking in the garden in the cool of the day, and the man and his wife hid themselves from the presence of the Lord God among the trees of the garden. But the Lord God called to the man and said to him, "Where are you?"
>
> —GENESIS 3:8–9

Notice that God asks them a question: "Where are you?" Because God is God, He doesn't ask questions because He lacks information. He asks them to give us revelation. He was fully aware that something had gone terribly wrong. Hiding behind trees wasn't and still isn't an effective plan when it comes to avoiding God's presence—He has X-ray vision.

In the aftermath of their fall, the ramifications of their decision became clear. Created to be the image-bearing co-regents of God on the earth, Adam and Eve shattered that image through their sin. Like looking into a broken mirror, the image was distorted and ugly. This was the genesis of identity confusion in the human heart. Since this moment, mankind has become susceptible to the lie that our identity is shaped by our twisted desires, shameful decisions, or painful pasts. Adam and Eve lost the awareness of God's goodness, and their eyes had become opened wide to their own shame.

When God created Adam and Eve and gave them their authority, they thrived in every endeavor. Naming the animals, cultivating and keeping the garden, and representing the Lord God to the rest of creation—everything they did flourished, including themselves. Their relationship with the Lord was consistent and intimate. There was nothing broken, nothing missing, and nothing shameful. It was perfectly peaceful and full of the shalom (peace) of God.

Because they rejected God's commands and decided to believe the lie, instead of grace for success upon their lives, there was a curse. Instead of intimacy, there was isolation and hiddenness. This curse affected the natural order of creation by introducing death, division, and disease even unto the ground they walked on. Instead of the land easily yielding fruit, cultivation to ensure fruitfulness would require Adam's blood, sweat, and tears, while waging a constant battle with thorns and thistles.

> "Cursed is the ground because of you; in pain you shall eat of it
> all the days of your life; thorns and thistles it shall bring forth
> for you; and you shall eat the plants of the field. By the sweat
> of your face you shall eat bread, till you return to the ground."
> —GENESIS 3:17–19

Failure and poverty were not an original part of human DNA. They were not part of God's original design. They came as a result of our sin. The injustice and poverty that exists in the world should serve as a constant reminder that man's decisions have led to hardship and destruction.

Instead of asking God why He would allow this, we must consider that we are the authors of our own failures.

The ultimate impact of their fall was the introduction of death. Adam would live over nine hundred years upon the earth, but death set in immediately. God never created human beings to die. Death is a completely unnatural condition for humans. Before the fall, mankind was clothed with the glory and the life of God. It wasn't until Adam and Eve's act of disobedience that they realized that they were naked, stripped of life. The onset of disease began that day—disease of the body and the soul. Mankind immediately began to degenerate and weaken.

Eventually, death would kill them physically, but it also infected every other facet of their life. Even though they were physically still alive on the day they sinned, death, like a disease, began its takeover. It showed up in their relationship with Father God, separating them from the giver of life and breaking their sweet fellowship with Him in the garden. It also came to bear on their marital relationship. No longer were they working in partnership with each other, under the authority of heaven. Instead, they were striving against one another. Competition, domination, unmet needs, and lack of communication all found their diabolical birth in the fall.

"Your desire shall be for your husband, and he shall rule over you."
—GENESIS 3:16

The gift of sex within marriage, like everything else God created as good and perfect, was also corrupted. We are still seeing the massive brokenness of human sexuality proliferating throughout our world. Instead of it producing fruitfulness and multiplication in the safety of the nuclear family, we see the devil's mutilation of human dignity and sexual purity. What God intended to be a natural, pleasurable bonding between a man and his wife that would produce offspring has become animalistic and recreational. Like everything else God created, sex was created to produce life and fruitfulness, but the fall twisted this and, further, it caused childbirth to become difficult and painful for woman.

"I will surely multiply your pain in child-bearing; in pain you shall bring forth children."
—v. 16

The final blow was dealt when Adam and Eve were escorted out of the Garden of Eden and sent out into the uncultivated, cursed earth to fend for themselves.

> Then the LORD God said, "Behold, the man has become like one of Us, to know good and evil. And now, lest he put out his hand and take also of the tree of life, and eat, and live forever"— therefore the Lord God sent him out of the garden of Eden to till the ground from which he was taken. So He drove out the man; and He placed cherubim at the east of the garden of Eden, and a flaming sword which turned every way, to guard the way to the tree of life.
> —GENESIS 3:22–24, NKJV

No longer were they living in paradise with everything they would need to thrive at their fingertips. No longer were they confident in their approach and access to the Lord. Instead, they were banished and alone. God's decision to move them out of Eden was actually a merciful move. Had He left them with the ability to reenter the garden in their sinful state, they may have eaten from the Tree of Life and become irreparably damaged and lost. So, as the verse says, God placed an angel at the entrance to protect them from destroying themselves before God could redeem mankind back to Himself. Those whom God had created to have dominion were now wanderers. Mankind was originally fashioned to flourish but now had fallen. God's son and daughter were slaves, sold out by a liar, and instead of being filled with glory, they were now overwhelmed with guilt.

Chapter Four
REDEEMED TO FLOURISH

The gospel is often called the Good News. This is how Jesus declared it as He used His reading from the prophet Isaiah as His announcement of His ministry on Earth:

> The Spirit of the Lord is upon me, because he has anointed me to proclaim good news to the poor. He has sent me to proclaim liberty to the captives and recovering of sight to the blind, to set at liberty those who are oppressed to proclaim the year of the Lord's favor.
>
> —LUKE 4:18–19

The Good News of the gospel message that Jesus went forth declaring drew thousands of broken, helpless, and infirmed people. Everywhere He went preaching, the crowds were overwhelming. Thousands of people lined the streets and filled every available space to hear Jesus preach the Good News.

One of the most powerful messages that Jesus ever preached was the parable of the lost son, commonly called the Prodigal Son. The story is so powerful because it portrays the fall of man so uniquely and uses such emotional language, which gives us an intimate picture of the true heart of God as a father. Let's read it together now.

> A certain man had two sons. And the younger of them said to his father, "Father, give me the portion of goods that falls to me." So he divided to them his livelihood. And not many days after, the younger son gathered all together, journeyed to a far country, and there wasted his possessions with prodigal living. But when he had spent all, there arose a severe famine in that land, and he began to be in want. Then he went and joined himself to a citizen of that country, and he sent him into his fields to feed swine. And he would gladly have filled his stomach with the pods that the swine ate, and no one gave him anything.
> But when he came to himself, he said, "How many of my father's hired servants have bread enough and to spare, and I

perish with hunger! I will arise and go to my father, and will say to him, 'Father, I have sinned against heaven and before you, and I am no longer worthy to be called your son. Make me like one of your hired servants.'"

And he arose and came to his father. But when he was still a great way off, his father saw him and had compassion, and ran and fell on his neck and kissed him. And the son said to him, "Father, I have sinned against heaven and in your sight, and am no longer worthy to be called your son."

But the father said to his servants, "Bring out the best robe and put it on him, and put a ring on his hand and sandals on his feet. And bring the fatted calf here and kill it, and let us eat and be merry; for this my son was dead and is alive again; he was lost and is found."

—LUKE 15:11–24, NKJV

The parable clearly lays out the fall of man and the posture of the Father, waiting and looking for the moment of redemption. The son went off into the world looking to fulfill his selfish desires, lured by the siren calls of sin. The Father didn't restrain him but allowed him to go, knowing that nothing but disappointment and pain awaited his son.

Wise in his own mind, the son wasted his inheritance to the point that he ended up in servitude and eating from the pen of swine, the most unclean animal from a Jewish perspective. This was the ultimate low. Everything was wasted—his identity, inheritance, and freedom. Through his actions, the son had declared that he was dead to his father and his father was dead to him. Yet, in a moment of desperation, he remembered what had been lost and how good it was in the Father's house. I don't believe he dared to think that he deserved a second chance. He merely realized that, if he was going to be a slave, at least he could be a slave in his father's house, where even they had it better than he did at that moment. He had fallen so far. He used to be a son in charge of everything. Now the best he could see for himself was going back home and begging his father to let him be a slave.

The next part of the story is the most powerful. The father saw the son approaching his home from a long way off. This perfectly describes our journey to the Father. We have spent it all and are so far from where we were created and purposed to live. But the Father has never taken His eye off of us. He has never given up on redeeming us back to Himself.

Once the father in Jesus's parable saw his son approaching in his filthy, sin-ridden garments, the father did the unthinkable. He lifted up the bulk of his garments, exposing his legs, and ran toward the son. Such an act was considered shameful in Middle Eastern culture. A man of stature would never expose his legs nor would he be seen running. Jesus's listeners would have been shocked to hear of such a display by a scorned father.

Once the father reached his son, he didn't strike the shameful son with his hand, and he didn't demand that he leave in shame. That is the way the listener would have expected the story to go. Instead, with tears spilling from his eyes, this impassioned father *fell* on his son's neck and kissed him. This father's falling onto the neck of his broken son was more powerful than the fall the son took into the mire of the pig pen. When the son asked for forgiveness and confessed his sin against his father, he didn't ask for reinstatement. That would've been unthinkable. He instead begged for the concession to be a slave—a hired hand. He was hoping that somehow his father would have a modicum of sympathy remaining in his heart toward him.

As if the story couldn't get any more astonishing, what Jesus described the Father doing next illustrates the beauty of redemption.

> Bring out the best robe and put it on him, and put a ring on his hand and sandals on his feet. And bring the fatted calf here and kill it, and let us eat and be merry; for this my son was dead and is alive again; he was lost and is found.
>
> —vv. 22–23, NKJV

Redeemed and Restored

This story is so powerful because it profoundly depicts what Jesus knew about the Father's intentions toward the lost. This is why God sent His Son to the earth: to redeem and restore that which was lost back to its original place and purpose.

Jesus's death upon the cross would pay the price for the sins of the world that the world could never pay. Instead of leaving us in the state of spiritual death and separation, He devised a plan in eternity with the Son and the Holy Spirit to redeem humanity back to Himself. In this plan, Jesus would take on human flesh and step into history to redeem and restore back to sonship those who believe in Him.

> And Jesus said to him, "Today salvation has come to this house, because he also is a son of Abraham; for the son of Man has come to seek and save that which was lost."
>
> —LUKE 19:9–10, NKJV

> "For God so loved the world that he gave his only begotten son, that whoever believes in Him should not perish but have everlasting life. For God did not send His Son into the world to condemn the world, but that the world through Him might be saved."
>
> —JOHN 3:16–17, NKJV

The word *redeem* means much more than just being rescued. It is a word that has legal implications. It means to "purchase back" or "reclaim." Many times, this word is used in relation to indentured slaves. For example, indentured slaves could buy back their freedom. Or, in another example, if a landowner had put his land up as collateral, he could redeem back that land once he had sufficient means. In the case of the prodigal and in our own stories, there was no possibility of redemption on our own terms. It took action of a divine, supernatural nature to initiate our redemption. It took God's intervention—His paying our debt—so we could come home once again. Jesus willingly paid the price for our sin and redeemed us back to the Father.

> In Him we have redemption through His blood, the forgiveness of sins, according to the riches of His grace.
>
> —EPHESIANS 1:7, NKJV

> ...knowing that you were not redeemed with corruptible things, like silver or gold, from your aimless conduct received by tradition from your fathers, but with the precious blood of Christ, as a lamb without blemish and without spot.
>
> —1 PETER 1:18–19, NKJV

There is a significant difference between redemption and restoration. To redeem something, as we previously stated, is to buy something back. But to restore something is a step further. To restore means "to bring back or reinstate something to its original state." The parable of the lost son doesn't just teach redemption, but it also portrays God as a father who completely restores his son back to his original place in the family. This is why the message of the cross is called Good News and also why it is so scandalous.

The Reckless Love of God

Two of the worship leaders at Radiant, the church my wife, Jane, and I planted over twenty-two years ago, wrote a song together that was released in 2018 called "Reckless Love." The first time I heard it, it was during a night of worship and prayer. The words struck me so strongly that I knew I was hearing more than a song. I was hearing an anthem of heaven that would change a generation. That may sound grandiose, but having heard a lot of worship songs over the years, I have never been so impacted by a song. Cory Asbury and Caleb Culver's song would be an unvarnished version of God's amazing grace, melodically telling the story of the lengths that God was willing to go to redeem and restore us.

When Cory released his album, the song had already experienced a groundswell due to its being sung by Stephanie Gretzinger live at Bethel and posted on their YouTube channel. For several months, this song was at the top of radio play and, for a time, was the number-one streamed song on Spotify. Justin Bieber played it live at a secular music festival during an impromptu worship gathering. The lyrics powerfully portray the passionate pursuit of a single-minded and focused father, dead-set on winning back the apple of His eye.

> Before I spoke a word, You were singing over me
> You have been so, so good to me
> Before I took a breath, You breathed Your life in me
> You have been so, so kind to me
> Oh, the overwhelming, never-ending, reckless love of God
> Oh, it chases me down, fights till I'm found, leaves the
> ninety-nine
> I couldn't earn it, and I don't deserve it.

Still You give Yourself away
Oh, the overwhelming, never-ending, reckless love of God
When I was Your foe, still Your love fought for me
You have been so, so good to me
When I felt no worth, You paid it all for me
You have been so, so kind to me
And oh, the overwhelming, never-ending, reckless love
   of God
Oh, it chases me down, fights 'til I'm found, leaves the
   ninety-nine
And I couldn't earn it; I don't deserve it.
Still You give Yourself away
Oh, the overwhelming, never ending, reckless love of God.[1]

I believe this song is resonating with this generation because, more than ever, we can identify with the prodigal son and we long for the love of the Father. The Holy Spirit used Cory and Caleb to release a song from the heart of the Father over a generation.

God wants to unveil a revelation of His heart toward a broken and sinful world that is searching for love and life. He also wants to reveal the whole truth about the spiritual inheritance awaiting His children who have freely received Christ. He is not content to make us His servants. He calls us sons and daughters, firstborn, and welcomed back to the Father's household with all things that were lost being completely restored to us.

Restored to Flourishing

In our story, the father called for the servants to bring out a fresh robe, a new ring, and clean sandals. This is where we can see the parallel Jesus was drawing in reference to the things lost in the fall. He was using this parable to help us understand that all those things are being restored by what He would accomplish on the cross for our salvation. This restoration could not have been accomplished by our great efforts or by us somehow earning the right to get back what was lost. It is completely and utterly the radical love of God that has granted a gift so ridiculous, only a fictional parable could portray its lengths, depth, width, and breadth.

The robe that the father put on his son is a picture of our righteousness before God. In Christ, we are no longer seen by God in the rags of our sin but clothed in the righteousness of God that was purchased by Jesus on our behalf. We are clothed in spotless, beautiful garments that we could not earn and do not deserve.

> I am overwhelmed with joy in the LORD my God! For he has dressed me with the clothing of salvation and draped me in a robe of righteousness. I am like a bridegroom in his wedding suit or a bride with her jewels.
> —ISAIAH 61:10, NLT

> For He made Him who knew no sin to be sin for us, that we might become the righteousness of God in Him.
> —2 CORINTHIANS 5:21, NKJV

The rags of our own righteousness could never compare to the new nature that we receive when we turn back to the Father and fall upon His mercy and forgiveness. He doesn't just clean us up or launder our old garments. He replaces them with a righteousness that is not our own.

> But we are all like an unclean thing, and all our righteousness are like filthy rags.
> —ISAIAH 64:6, NKJV

> Yet indeed I also count all things loss, for the excellence of the knowledge of Christ Jesus my Lord, for whom I have suffered the loss of all things, and count them as rubbish that I may gain Christ. And be found in Him, not having my own righteousness, which is from the Law, but that which is from God by faith.
> —PHILIPPIANS 3:8–9, NKJV

He clothes us in a righteousness so rich and so pure, we could never earn it or deserve it. It is this new robe of righteousness that God the Father sees every time He looks at us. He can no longer see the old tattered reminders of our rebellion. He can only see the shining new nature that was gifted to us from God's heavenly grace.

A New Ring

In the garden, God had originally given regal authority to Adam. Adam's job was to be a viceroy of heaven, exercising complete authority over every aspect of God's good creation. He had literally been given a dominion mandate from God the Father. It was from this place of authority that Adam was invited by God to name each of the animals and given the task to cultivate the garden and expand its borders into all the earth.

> Then God said, "Let Us make man in Our image, according to Our likeness; let them have dominion over the fish of the sea, over the birds of the air, and over the cattle, over all the earth and over every creeping thing that creeps on the earth."
> —GENESIS 1:26, NKJV

When Adam chose to believe the word of the deceiver over the word of the Lord God, He in essence became a vessel of Satan and yielded the God-given authority of the earth to him. Once a son with the Father's ring of authority, Adam had become indentured into slavery by his own will. This transference of authority is the reason Satan operates in this world with such power. It was never meant to be this way.

Satan flaunted his authority when he appeared before Jesus in the wilderness to tempt him. Satan showed Jesus all the kingdoms of the world and offered them to Him, stating, "All this authority I will give You, and their glory; for this has been delivered to me and I give it to whomever I wish" (Luke 4:6, NKJV).

Where did Satan receive this authority over the kingdoms of the world? He got it in the garden, at the Tree of Knowledge of Good and Evil, by deceptive means. This is one of the reasons why the incarnation of Jesus was so important. Choosing to step into history in the form of humanity, retrace the steps of the original Adam without sin, and ultimately pay for the sins of humanity on the cross with His spotless blood, Jesus defeated the god of this world (a title the apostle Paul gave to Satan in 2 Corinthians 4:4) and took back the legal right to the authority lost by the first Adam. This is why we state emphatically that Jesus is Lord! Jesus now has all authority in heaven and on Earth. He has stripped the enemy of his authority and reinstituted the dominion mandate to those enslaved by sin. Now we are once again made sons and daughters through our acceptance and faith in Christ's redemptive work on the cross.

"All authority has been given to Me in heaven and on earth. Go therefore, and make disciples of all nations, baptizing them in the name of the Father, and of the Son and of the Holy Spirit."
—MATTHEW 28:18–19, NKJV

This truth is reflected in the parable of the prodigal son. The father doesn't just receive the son back as a slave or even just give him room and board. He puts a new ring on his son's finger. The signet ring in Near Eastern first-century culture was more than a valuable piece of jewelry or decoration. It was used to give or delegate authority. With this ring, one is able to sign legal documents on behalf of someone else and access their wealth. It is like having power of attorney.

When the father gave the returning son his ring, he was giving back to his son everything that his son had wasted in the world. The father was making a statement that they were back in business partnership together and everything that he owned also belonged once again to his son. The father was communicating that he completely trusted his son.

What a powerful picture of what the Father bestows upon us at the moment of our conversion. If we could only see through the eyes of the Spirit, we would realize the power and authority we carry in Christ Jesus. Each of God's children are restored to the family business of dominion. We have been given authority over the devil, demons, and disease. Then we are commissioned to go out in our Father's name to bring the created world, that has been under the sway of diabolical destruction, back into alignment with God's perfect purposes. This is the essence of what "on earth as it is in heaven" means. (See Matthew 6:10.)

The Sandals

Sandals were extremely necessary for living in the rough terrain of the Middle East. The very poor could not afford them, but most everyone else would sacrifice much in order to protect their feet from the rocky and jagged paths and roads that were traveled on foot. This returning son had gone from dressing in the finest garments to living in a pig pen and begging for the leftovers of their slop. He was also barefoot. He had left home with a skip in his step as he imagined all of the adventures he would experience in the world, and now returned with bare and bleeding feet, barely able to stand in his father's shadow. His journey home had been painful and scarring, but his father would not allow his shame to go on any longer.

New sandals speak of a new beginning and a new way of walking. It's a picture of God's grace—grace that covers and heals the scars of the past and grace that leads us forward on a new path of following Jesus. Every one of the disciples who followed Jesus were summoned to leave the old behind with two simple words: follow me. The journey that their decision would take them on was completely unknown to them at the time they gave their yes, but they found their purpose on Jesus's path.

> Therefore, as you received Christ Jesus the Lord, so walk in him.
> —COLOSSIANS 2:6 ESV

Our ability to walk with God has been restored. We are no longer left to walk in disgrace; we can now walk in the Spirit and in obedience to the Father. The feet that used to lead us into the snares of the devil are now beautiful, because they are now shod with the preparation of the gospel of peace (Ephesians 6:14).

Once we have been restored to life in Christ from our state of spiritual death, we will never be able to walk the same again. We have gone from wandering in the wastelands of hopelessness to being welcomed into the household of faith, where we can learn to flourish in the Father's house once again.

It's in Your Genes

A while ago, I took one of those DNA tests that give you a breakdown of your genetic background. I have always been curious about my heritage, but there were some family stories that I was hoping would be sorted out once and for all. On my dad's side, I had heard all my life that we were of Irish descent. On my mother's side, the story that was repeated often was my great-great-grandfather was either full-blooded Shawnee or was married to one. It's amazing that, over the last several years, the scientific ability to see our genetic code broken down for us has become mainstream.

When I got my results back several weeks later, there were some things that were expected in my breakdown, but also a few surprises. For one, the test showed that I have absolutely zero Native American genes. My family might have been exaggerating, but they were for sure not Shawnee. There was a significant amount of British and Irish in our family genes but not necessarily all Irish, which isn't uncommon among the British Isles. The stunner? I was about 3 percent Ashkenazi Jewish! I had no idea before this that I had any Jewish ancestry, but when I found this out, it thrilled my heart. The results traced it all the way back to a fourth or fifth grandparent who would've been 100 percent Jewish.

It is truly amazing how much you can find in your DNA that you didn't know was there. Doctors and scientists are able to look at the genetic code written in every cell of our bodies and determine every detail about our beings, and disorders we are susceptible to. Genetic engineering is one of the most cutting-edge frontiers in the world of disease prevention and biology. Paternity tests have also made it possible to reconnect long-lost families and solve mysteries that before would have been left unsolved. It's all in the genes!

If this is true of our physical being, are there similarities in the realm of the spirit? Absolutely. When we are born again, we receive brand-new natures and genetic compositions of our souls. More than just being forgiven, we are remade into new creations, by the power of God's Word. This new reality is more than mere words or metaphors; we are spiritually transformed.

> ...having been born again, not of corruptible seed but incorruptible, through the word of God which lives and abides forever.
> —1 PETER 1:23, NKJV

The word that Peter uses for "seed" in this verse is the Greek word *sporos*. It comes from the same word we translate into English as "spore" or "seed that is sown." As we know, a seed is a carrier of genetic code. God designed everything He created with a seed in it, so that it would produce after its own kind and multiply. The discovery of DNA and the genetic map took man thousands of years to see what God hardwired into everything under the sun.

> Then God said, "Let the earth bring forth grass, the herb that yields seed, and the fruit tree that yields fruit according to its kind, whose seed is in itself, on the earth"; and it was so. And

the earth brought forth grass, the herb that yields seed according to its kind, and the tree that yields fruit, whose seed is in itself according to its kind. And God saw that it was good.

—GENESIS 1:11–12, NKJV

Because of this, oranges reproduce oranges. Wheat reproduces wheat. Birds reproduce birds. Humans reproduce humans. The divine nature of God carried in His word produces Godlike righteousness. In other words, the nature or image of God that was broken because of sin is ultimately restored through Jesus Christ.

As with every seed, the potential that it holds only becomes realized when the seed is received into the soil. It is this act that releases and activates the seed to begin production. In the same way, our faith in Jesus's finished work on the cross and His resurrection from the dead is the act of receiving the seed. Once the message of the gospel is received by faith, new life takes root, and we receive a new, divine nature.

Return to Flourishing

The final step in the father's embrace of his returning son was to call for his servants to prepare a feast back at his home, "for this my son," he said, "was dead, and is alive again. He was lost, and is found" (Luke 15:24). What a beautiful portrayal of the joy the father felt as he received his son back from the loss that was even unto death.

This is also a powerful description of our deliverance from darkness into the kingdom of God. Not only does the Father forgive us and restore all that was wasted, but He prepares a feast in His house in our honor. There is found a place at the Father's table for us once again. We are not assigned to be servants who live outside the home, but we are brought in as sons where the tears of intercession are replaced by shouts of joy and celebration.

In a very real sense, we have been brought back into the garden, and our relationship with Father God has been restored. We are now invited to eat of the Tree of Life, the fruit of the cross, and receive eternal life because Jesus, the second Adam, has overcome and made a way for us to come home.

In less than twenty-four hours, the prodigal son had gone from begging for pig slop to feasting in his father's house once again. He who was impoverished in body and spirit by his own rebellion and sin was completely restored to his family and returned to the environment that he was designed to flourish in. And just like him, in one moment of repentance and faith toward Christ, each of us wayward sons and daughters are invited home by a gracious Father whose reckless love has never stopped pursuing us.

> Remember that you were at that time separated from Christ, alienated from the commonwealth of Israel and strangers to the covenants of promise, having no hope and without God in the world. But now in Christ Jesus you who once were far off have been brought near by the blood of Christ.
> For he himself is our peace, who has made us both one and has broken down in his flesh the dividing wall of hostility by abolishing the law of commandments expressed in ordinances, that he might create in himself one new man in place of the two, so making peace, and might reconcile us both to God in one body through the cross, thereby killing the hostility. And he came and preached peace to you who were far off and peace to those who were near. For through him we both have access in one Spirit to the Father.
> So then you are no longer strangers and aliens, but you are fellow citizens with the saints and members of the household of God, built on the foundation of the apostles and prophets, Christ Jesus himself being the cornerstone, in whom the whole structure, being joined together, grows into a holy temple in the Lord. In him you also are being built together into a dwelling place for God by the Spirit.
> —EPHESIANS 2:12–22

We may have felt hopeless and isolated in the state of sin, but in the kingdom of God, we have been made family and part of something so much bigger than ourselves. The current state of the culture around us wants to convince us that everything we are looking for is found out in the wildness of the world, and that, if we forego the pleasures it offers, that we will be far less than we could be, but nothing could be further from the truth.

The real party is going on in the Father's house, where His redeemed and restored children are feasting. They are not there alone, but the Father, the Son, and the Holy Spirit are there, whirling and reveling in the praise of the saints. The church is the house of God where prodigals are welcomed with kisses on the neck and restored back to their rightful places no matter how bad their pasts are. The church is an environment of praise, provision, and power, and it happens to be God's favorite place in the universe.

Chapter Five
ANOINTED TO FLOURISH

I must confess I don't have a clue about how the price of gasoline is determined. The last time I went to the gas station to fill up, I saw that the price of a gallon of gas was about three dollars. If you were to ask me how much a barrel of crude is selling for on the international market, I couldn't give you an answer. One time, I asked a guy in our church who works in commodities and seemed to understand how that kind of thing works. He gave me what I am sure he thought was a layman's explanation, but after I shook my head, pretending to get it, I walked away just as ignorant as I was before I had asked.

Even though the bigger, global perspective on big oil affected my drive to work every single day, my understanding was still limited. I could not grasp the bigger picture.

When it comes to understanding the anointing, many in the church are in the same position. When we talk about someone being anointed, we have a basic understanding of what that means: talented, gifted, or seemingly graced in a unique way by God to accomplish a purpose for God. We see it in an individualistic, practical manner. Most of the time when we talk about the anointing, we associate it with a special touch upon something or someone from heaven. Whether it is a sermon, preacher, worship leader, or special service, we understand the anointing to be localized. But the anointing also has a bigger, more corporate component that is seldom referred to or understood.

Understanding What Anointing Is

The Bible connects the idea of anointing with oil (olive oil specifically). The actual word used in the Hebrew Old Testament for *anoint* or *anointed* means "to smear or pour over with oil" and is the base word for where we get *Messiah*, meaning "the anointed one." Oil is a physical expression of transference of spiritual authority and power. It was used in the Old Testament to consecrate those things and people that were designated for the Lord's house and His purposes.

Then Moses took the anointing oil and anointed the tabernacle and all that was in it, and consecrated them. And he sprinkled some of it on the altar seven times, and anointed the altar and all its utensils and the basin and its stand, to consecrate them. And he poured some of the anointing oil on Aaron's head and anointed him to consecrate him.

—LEVITICUS 8:10–12

"And Aaron and his sons you shall bring to the door of the tabernacle of meeting, and you shall wash them with water. Then you shall take the garments, put the tunic on Aaron, and the robe of the ephod, the ephod, and the breastplate, and gird him with the intricately woven band of the ephod. You shall put the turban on his head, and put the holy crown on the turban. *And you shall take the anointing oil, pour it on his head, and anoint him.* Then you shall bring his sons and put tunics on them. And you shall gird them with sashes, Aaron and his sons, and put the hats on them. The priesthood shall be theirs for a perpetual statute. So you shall consecrate Aaron and his sons."

—EXODUS 29:4–9, NKJV, EMPHASIS ADDED

The anointing oil was also poured over the heads of kings, such as in the case of David by the prophet Samuel to indicate that he was God's choice to be the leader over his people Israel instead of the people's choice, Saul.

And the LORD said, "Arise, anoint him, for this is he." Then Samuel took the horn of oil and anointed him in the midst of his brothers. And the Spirit of the LORD rushed upon David from that day forward. And Samuel rose up and went to Ramah.

—1 SAMUEL 16:12–13

While an intensive study of the anointing in the Old Testament is intriguing and even tempting to divert into at this point, instead I want to draw your attention to a few significant distinctives about David's anointing which, I believe, serve to give us greater understanding of God's intentions for each of us.

First, notice that, when Samuel anointed David, he did it differently than he did with Saul. In David's case, it says that Samuel took a "horn of oil" as opposed to the "flask of oil" that he used earlier in anointing Saul.

(See 1 Samuel 10:1.) Why is this? A flask is a manmade object used to carry the anointing oil, just like Saul was a manmade leader. He was everything the people of Israel wanted in a king. Outwardly he was impressive, but internally he was corrupt and insecure.

> There was a man of Benjamin whose name was Kish, the son of Abiel, son of Zeror, son of Becorath, son of Aphiah, a Benjaminite, a man of wealth. And he had a son whose name was Saul, a handsome young man. There was not a man among the people of Israel more handsome than he. From his shoulders upward he was taller than any of the people.
>
> —1 SAMUEL 9:1–2

Saul was the people's choice, not God's. He was a mirror reflection of their own carnality and insecurity. I believe this is why Samuel used a manmade flask to anoint Saul. The horn of oil used in David's anointing was not made by human hands, which I will explain in just a minute. My point here is that, because Saul's process to becoming king was all man-made, once the oil flowed over Saul's head, there was an empowerment, but that smearing of power and authority could not cover the fear and lack of integrity in his heart.

There was a time when Saul ran into a school of prophets and he came under the influence of their corporate anointing. It is the only time in Saul's life, that we know of, where he prophesied. This is a powerful picture of the larger idea that we are trying to convey in this chapter. There is a distinct difference between an individual anointing upon a person and a corporate anointing upon a people joined together.

> Then he also went to Ramah, and came to the great well that is at Sechu. So he asked, and said, "Where are Samuel and David?" And someone said, "Indeed they are at Naioth in Ramah." So he went there to Naioth in Ramah. Then the Spirit of God was upon him also, and he went on and prophesied until he came to Naioth in Ramah. And he also stripped off his clothes and prophesied before Samuel in like manner, and lay down naked all that day and all that night. Therefore they say, "Is Saul also among the prophets?"
>
> —1 SAMUEL 19:22–24, NKJV

It was the spiritual environment that had been created in the spirit by the school of prophets that influenced Saul's messengers before him and, ultimately, the king himself.

Contrast Saul's anointing with David's. David was everything that Saul wasn't. He wasn't the popular, out front, obvious leader type in the eyes of men. He was even overlooked by his own father when the prophet came to inspect his other sons to see who among the sons of Jesse God had selected to lead His people. The Lord even warned Samuel not to "look on his appearance or on the height of his stature, because I have rejected him (Eliab). For the Lord sees not as man sees; man looks on the outward appearance, but the Lord looks on the heart" (1 Sam. 16:7).

After turning away each of Jesse's other sons, Samuel finally sees David as he comes in from keeping his father's sheep. Immediately, the Lord speaks to Samuel's heart to "arise, anoint him, for this is he. Then Samuel took the horn of oil and anointed him in the midst of his brothers. And the Spirit of the Lord rushed upon David from that day forward" (1 Sam. 16:12–13).

The horn is significant in the story. A horn is a supernatural vessel; one crafted by the Lord's magnificent design of the animal, most often a Ram, to which it belonged. Just as the Lord, at Creation, formed every part of an animal uniquely to reflect His wisdom and artistry, He uses His anointing to enhance His unique design for each person that it comes upon.

When Samuel uses a horn full of oil, it is a picture of God's sovereign choice of David, to set him apart for His purposes. This is further developed when we read that the Holy Spirit rushed upon David from that moment forward. Those words were not written about Saul at his anointing. Only a question was asked about Saul: "Has not the Lord anointed a prince over his people Israel?" (1 Sam. 10:1).

This is quite different than the Spirit of God confirming this moment. When we talk about the connection between the physical smearing or pouring of oil upon someone and the tangible presence, power, and purpose of God, one doesn't always guarantee the other. It is possible to go through the motions externally but not have a corresponding empowerment of God's favor spiritually. It isn't the oil that makes something holy or acceptable; it is the purpose of God that intersects with the faith of God's people, resulting in physical demonstrations of faith and worship.

David's life was shaped from the moment he experienced the anointing coming upon him. He had spent all those years minding the sheep out in the pasture with no audience or accolades, fending off predators and honing his skills with the sling and the lyre. The psalmist of Israel learned to access the presence of the Lord in worship in the obscurity of a shepherd's cave. Singing for an audience of One shaped David's understanding of the goodness of God. Recorded in the pages of inspired canon now, the songs that flowed from revelation and prayer began as his cries for help and shouts of celebration.

His hidden years of exile also formed the understanding of intimacy with God that so marked David's life. In the hardest times of his life, David did not turn away from the Lord in bitterness and confusion. Instead, he pressed deeper, searching out the Lord as his only refuge and stronghold. He didn't allow the questions or apparent absence of God to separate him, but he became a pursuer of God's presence. His songs ripped open the heavens and gave him access to God's divine protection, strength and security.

David was shaped by his pain, but pain that turned him towards the Lord in hopeful worship and raw honesty. In his desperation, he somehow grasped the idea that God was magnetically attracted to certain heart conditions and specific environments in the spirit.

Three Dimensions of the Anointing

Having established a baseline understanding of what the anointing is—the smearing or pouring out of God's presence, power, and favor to give us supernatural empowerment to accomplish His purpose—it is equally important that we understand the different ways that the anointing is released. As we have seen in the Old Testament examples, God calls for anything sacred that has been set apart for His unique purposes of worship to be anointed: utensils in the temple, prophets, priests, and kings. In the Old Testament, with a few exceptions, these are the primary objects of God's anointing on an individual level. These anointings are very specifically given according to the calling upon the person's life.

In the New Testament, the concept of the anointing is further developed and brought to its fullness in the person of Jesus the Christ or Anointed

One. As was stated earlier, the word *Messiah* comes from the Hebrew word for "anointed." As the apostles began to proclaim Jesus as Messiah to a primarily Greek-speaking world, they translated these Hebrew, Old Testament concepts so that those to whom they ministered could receive and understand the testimony of Jesus Christ. The closest equivalent word for "Messiah" or "Anointed One" in the Greek language is *Christos*, which is where we get our English word *Christ*. We will talk more about Jesus, the Anointed One, as the prototype of walking in the anointing in the next chapter. What is important for now is that we have a clear understanding of the three dimensions of the anointing revealed in the New Testament. Let's take a look at each of these briefly.

1. An individual anointing

The first dimension of the anointing is what we will call the individual anointing. An individual anointing is simply recognizing that every born-again Christian has received the indwelling presence of the Holy Spirit and, therefore, is grafted into the body of Christ (the Anointed One), which gives them access to the same anointing of the Holy Spirit that Jesus had in the flesh. We have literally received the smearing or outpouring of God's tangible, abiding presence when we accept Jesus into our lives.

In the Old Testament, God's divine presence dwelt in the earthly tabernacle in the holy of holies. In the New Testament, the fullness of that type has now come to pass and the presence of God dwells in the holy of holies of our hearts as we ourselves are the temple of God. Paul's grand revelation of this is expressed throughout his letters, but never clearer than in 1 Corinthians 3:16:

> Do you not know that you are God's temple and that God's Spirit dwells in you?

This indwelling Holy Spirit is not just a theoretical statement, but a spiritual, practical reality for every believer. Paul states in 1 Corinthians 2:12–13 that "we have received not the spirit of the world, but the Spirit who is from God, that we might understand the things freely given us by God. And we impart this in words not taught by human wisdom but taught by the Spirit, interpreting spiritual truths to those who are spiritual."

At the moment we are born again, God gives us the gift of the Holy

Spirit to seal us as belonging to Him, affirm our sonship, and lead and guide us deeper into the truth of God's kingdom. He also comes to empower us with supernatural power and release spiritual gifts through each of us. This is part and parcel of our inheritance as children of God.

The apostle John, in his first epistle, wrote about this individual anointing in 1 John 2:20: "But you have an anointing from the Holy One, and you know all things..." (NKJV). He goes further in this teaching a few verses later:

> These things I have written to you concerning those who try to deceive you. But the anointing which you have received from Him abides in you, and you do not need that anyone teach you; but as the same anointing teaches you concerning all things, and is true, and is not a lie, and just as it has taught you, you will abide in Him.
>
> —vv. 26–27, NKJV

There are a few things here that I feel are significant for us to grasp. First, every Christian has an anointing. It is the presence of the great Helper, the Spirit of Truth Himself. Secondly, the purpose of this individual anointing is to lead and instruct us in our relationship with Jesus, the head of the body. The Holy Spirit, as Jesus promised, will lead us into all truth and will reveal Jesus to us in a deeper, more intimate fashion. Jesus doesn't just save us and keep us for heaven. He comes to us and gives us His anointing, by way of the divine Comforter and Counselor, to lead us and guide us. This is promised to each of His children.

> And I will pray the Father, and He will give you another Helper, that He may abide with you forever—the Spirit of truth, whom the world cannot receive, because it neither sees Him nor knows Him; but you know Him, for He dwells with you and will be in you. I will not leave you orphans; I will come to you.
>
> —JOHN 14:16–18, NKJV

> But the Helper, the Holy Spirit, whom the Father will send in My name, He will teach you all things, and bring to your remembrance all things that I said to you.
>
> —JOHN 14:26, NKJV

I still have many things to say to you, but you cannot bear them now. When the Spirit of truth comes, he will guide you into all truth, for he will not speak on his own authority but whatever he hears he will speak and he will declare to you the things that are to come.

—JOHN 16:12–14, ESV

In any discussion about the Holy Spirit and the anointing, it is important to start here, because so many Christians have a view of themselves that is different than God's view, and even hell's view of them. If we do not see ourselves as changed or empowered but merely sinners who have received grace and a place in heaven when we die, we will live far below our birthright. But if we can begin to gain a revelation that the greater One of God dwells within each of us and that we each have a portion or measure of the anointing, we will realize that, in the spirit, heaven sees the same oil dripping off of us as was present upon Jesus of Nazareth as He ascended from His Jordan River baptism. None of us have the Spirit without measure as Jesus did, but each of us has *a measure* of what Jesus did—and that's more than enough.

But to each one of us grace was given according to the measure of Christ's gift....

—EPHESIANS 4:7, NKJV

...as God has dealt to each one a measure of faith. For as we have many members in one body, but all members do not have the same function, so we, being many, are one body in Christ, and individually members of one another. Having then gifts differing according to the grace given to us, let us use them.

—ROMANS 12:3–6, NKJV

2. The specific anointing

While every believer has an individual anointing because of the presence of the Holy Spirit in their lives, there is also a specific anointing that is distinct and personally unique to each member. This aspect of the anointing is not so much about general confirmation and direction as it is a specific grace given according to the unique calling and function within the body of Christ and the purpose of God. Paul references this in Romans

12, as well as 1 Corinthians 12, as part of the revelation he received about the body of Christ. Certain graces and callings are given to each member to carry out the eternal purpose of God in the earth. The specific anointing is given in direct proportion to a specific calling.

Think of someone who has what we refer to as a "grace" upon their lives to live in a very difficult Third-World environment as a missionary. They are able to endure abject poverty and the lack of comforts that America would afford them because of a sense of divine call and accompanying grace. This is a specific anointing.

An anointing is different from just a talent or natural gifting. Talents are natural in their orientation. They are like seeds that can be developed and grown. A gift is something built into our natural personality or abilities.

An anointing, on the other hand, is supernatural in its orientation. Remember the word *anoint* means "the rubbing" or "the smearing." There has to be contact for *anointing* to take place. Oftentimes the concept of "anointing" is connected to the foundational doctrine of the laying on of hands. The laying on of hands is a doctrine that conveys transference of blessing, strength, or power. There has to be contact with the oil and the person who has the oil before there can be a transference. An anointing by God requires us to receive something that isn't ours in the first place. It is given after contact has been made.

Even though each person's anointing is different, or should we say, customized to the individual, we must be careful not to think that some are more important. Even though we may be tempted to glamorize some anointings such as missionaries, preachers, apostles, or worship leaders, the truth is there are specific and unique anointings upon each believer's life.

Paul highlighted the significance of each member and their anointing to the overall function and growth of the church:

> For as the body is one and has many members, but all the members of that one body, being many, are one body, so also is Christ. For by one Spirit we were all baptized into one body— whether Jews or Greeks, whether slaves or free—and have all been made to drink into one Spirit. For in fact the body is not one member but many.

If the foot should say, "Because I am not a hand, I am not of the body," is it therefore not of the body? And if the ear should say, "Because I am not an eye, I am not of the body," is it therefore not of the body? If the whole body were an eye, where would be the hearing? If the whole were hearing, where would be the smelling? But now God has set the members, each one of them, in the body just as He pleased.

—1 Corinthians 12:12–18, nkjv

In his letter to the Ephesians, Paul highlighted some very specific anointings that Christ gave to the church upon His ascension to the right hand of God the Father:

And He Himself gave some to be apostles, some prophets, some evangelists, and some pastors and teachers, for the equipping of the saints for the work of ministry, for the edifying of the body of Christ.

—Ephesians 4:11–12, nkjv

At the top of the list is apostles. The original twelve apostles are obvious in their anointing and supernatural grace upon their lives and ministries, but there are multiple others listed in the New Testament as apostles. Even though there is a large segment of the body of Christ that believes the office of apostle ceased with the death of the final of the twelve, church history demonstrates something different. Great leaders throughout the ages demonstrated apostolic influence and gifting. One such leader was John Wesley. The same could be said about prophets.

Although many modern-day theologians would argue that there are no longer any prophets in the church, that does not minimize the reality that God is still raising up men and women with a specific anointing aimed at bringing the body of Christ to a state of maturity. It is somewhat interesting to me that, in Western Christianity, we have basically built the foundation of our churches and denominations upon three out of the five ascension gift offices that Jesus gave. We are more than comfortable with pastors, teachers, and evangelists in our modern construct of Christianity, but are we missing a revelation that could launch the church to a place of greater unity, maturity, and power? I believe the answer is a resounding yes!

We will discuss the role of the apostle and prophet, along with the other fivefold ministry gifts later, but it is important to recognize that, not only have these specific anointings remained in the church up until this day, there is a specific purpose for these gifts. If we fail to recognize them and receive them, we will be stunted in our growth and limited in our progress both individually and corporately.

What about everyone else though? You may be thinking, *I am not an apostle* (that you know of) or *I can't prophesy* (that you know of). *Is there a specific anointing for me?*

Because I believe every believer has a specific, holy calling in Christ, I believe there is also a corresponding anointing for every believer. In fact, one of the beautiful aspects of the specific fivefold ministries is to help each believer discover and grow in their unique calling so that they can carry out the work of the ministry or service to the Lord.

It is beyond debate that, when Jesus saved you, He saved you from sin and hell, but as 2 Timothy 1:9 says, He also saved you unto a holy calling: "Who saved us and called us with a holy calling, not according to our works, but according to His own purpose and grace which was given to us in Christ Jesus before time began" (NKJV).

3. The corporate anointing

While many books have been written to help believers discover their own unique spiritual gifting and anointing, not much has been written about the corporate anointing. I believe it is a mystery that, once unlocked, gives us a greater understanding of the spiritual environment that is created when we come together in the Spirit as the body of Christ. Let me walk you back into the Psalms to show you some things about the corporate anointing.

God's Favorite Place

Psalm 87 has recently become one of my favorite psalms. There is so much revelation in the Book of Psalms that expresses the emotions of God in a way that other forms of biblical literature don't. The opening verses of this short psalm give us a big picture of God's favorite place on Earth.

On the holy mountain stands the city he founded; the Lord loves the gates of Zion more than all the dwelling places of Jacob. Glorious things are spoken of you, O city of God.

—PSALM 87:1–3

When the Bible, specifically the Old Testament, refers to Zion, in general it is speaking of the city of Jerusalem. But Zion is a specific sector of Jerusalem. It is a single hill just outside of the central city and the place David built his palace and called home. When David responded to the desire of his heart to bring the Ark of the Covenant back to the center of Israel's culture and worship, he did not usher it back to Gibeah where the Tabernacle of Moses was still in existence. Instead, he brought it into Jerusalem and right to Zion, next to the place where his palace had been established.

And they brought in the ark of God and set it inside the tent that David had pitched for it, and they offered burnt offerings and peace offerings before God.

—1 CHRONICLES 16:1

David wanted God's presence not just to be central to Israel but also close to his home. He built a tabernacle (a tent, really) with only one wide-open compartment and placed the ark in it. He also appointed musicians to minister to the Lord around the clock, prophesying and singing in the presence of God night and day.

So David left Asaph and his brothers there before the ark of the covenant of the Lord to minister regularly before the ark as each day required, and also Obed-edom and his sixty-eight brothers, while Obed-edom, the son of Jeduthun, and Hosah were to be gatekeepers. And he left Zadok the priest and his brothers the priests before the tabernacle of the Lord in the high place that was at Gibeon to offer burnt offerings to the Lord on the altar of burnt offering regularly morning and evening, to do all that is written in the Law of the Lord that he commanded Israel. With them were Heman and Jeduthun and the rest of those chosen and expressly named to give thanks to the Lord, for his steadfast love endures forever.

—1 CHRONICLES 16:37–41

This move violated every precept God had given to Moses about how to meticulously build the tabernacle, care for the ark, and appoint the priesthood. But for some reason God didn't mind. In fact, He really liked it.

Notice what the psalmist wrote: "The Lord loves the gates of Zion *more* than all dwelling places of Jacob" (Psalm 87:2, emphasis added). Jacob is the other name that God uses to describe His covenant people Israel. As new covenant believers who have been grafted into the Israel of God, this is a reference and promise to us as well. Just like natural Israel, the people of God have many dwelling places. In the church, we have many wonderful classes and resources that we produce. We have missions, outreaches, and social gatherings. We love to study God's Word by ourselves and in small groups. But there is one environment, one dwelling place of ours, that God is magnetically drawn to because of what it means—Zion.

Zion—the Gathered People of God

Zion is the place where all of God's people are intentionally gathered together to worship in unity with God's presence being the magnificent centerpiece. It is the corporate gathering place of the saints in expectant worship and adoration. It is in this environment that God releases the corporate oil or anointing in greater measure that causes "glorious things" to be spoken over the church. Zion is a way of describing the supernatural reality that takes place when His body is assembled in one place and around one purpose and pursuit.

> But you have come to Mount Zion and to the city of the living God, the heavenly Jerusalem, and to innumerable angels in festal gathering, and to the assembly of the firstborn who are enrolled in heaven, and to God, the judge of all, and to the spirits of the righteous made perfect.
> —Hebrews 12:22–23

Paul's writing about this mystery of the corporate anointing in Ephesians describes what takes place in the spirit as the church gathers together, in proper order, to worship Him in spirit and truth.

> In whom the whole building, being fitted together, grows into
> a holy temple in the Lord, in whom you also are being built
> together for a dwelling place of God in the Spirit.
> —Ephesians 2:21–22, nkjv

This is a powerful picture of heaven's vantage point when we are gathered. The collective gathering of measured anointing coming together in unity actually assembles the unified body of Christ in our midst. We each bring the unique part of the body that we represent, and together we re-present the fullness of Christ (the anointed one) back to the heavenly realms as well as the world.

God has refused to release the fullness of His anointing upon one human being like He did in the incarnation of Jesus, who had the Spirit without measure. But, instead, He has spread it to each individual member and reassembles it in a corporate setting as an expression of Himself. In this way, no one can take the credit, but instead all must give God the glory for His manifest presence. This is the environment of corporate oil.

I have literally walked into a worship gathering feeling discouraged and not wanting to worship or preach, only to be picked up and carried by the current of corporate anointing. I have seen hundreds of people experience healing for their bodies and souls in the midst of worship gatherings before even asking for someone to anoint them with oil and pray over them. How did this happen? They stepped into corporate oil, and Jesus touched them sovereignly. We vastly underestimate what is going on behind the veil of eternity in our environments. All we see are lights, people, and hands lifted. All we hear are melodies and beats and voices. Underneath all of this natural reality is a greater reality. There are ministering angels stirring the waters of healing and waging warfare against demonic oppression in people's lives. God Himself is singing over the top of us with songs of deliverance and joy.

> You are my hiding place; You shall preserve me from trouble;
> You shall surround me with songs of deliverance. Selah.
> —Psalm 32:7, nkjv

"The Lord your God is with you, the Mighty Warrior who saves. He will take great delight in you; in his love he will no longer rebuke you, but will rejoice over you with singing."

—ZEPHANIAH 3:17, NIV

God Enthroned

When Jesus taught us to pray "Thy kingdom come, Thy will be done on earth as it is in heaven" (Matthew 6:10, KJV), He wasn't teaching us an ethereal principle of well-wishing and good intentions. He literally meant what He was teaching.

God's desire is for His kingdom reality and His will to manifest exactly the same way on Earth as they continually occur in heaven. It's important for us to remember that not everything that happens on Earth or in our personal lives is God's will. We live in a fallen world that is in transition. Jesus's victorious resurrection has defeated death and inaugurated the beginning of God's redemption of His broken world. As it currently stands, we still live in the now and the not yet. This is where faith and prayer come in.

Jesus wants us to be aware that, even though there is brokenness, all around us, our prayers matter and have the ability to change the atmosphere and environments in which we find ourselves. This change comes in the spiritual before it ever manifests in the natural. The currency of heaven is faith, and the weapons of our warfare are spiritual. (See 2 Corinthians 10:4.)

David, as we have already mentioned, had a massive revelation of this and wrote something staggering in Psalm 22:3: "But you are holy, enthroned in the praises of Israel" (NKJV) The keyword is *enthroned*. The only person who sits on a throne is a king or monarch. The throne that David described is not a physical throne, but a spiritual reality that is created by our physical obedience, presence, and praises.

Our corporate worship, as the people of God, creates an environment in the Spirit that can only be described as a throne. I believe the picture this is painting is that, when God's people gather in worship, the spiritual atmosphere is shifted so much that the King enters it as His resting place from which to declare and enforce His regal will. It becomes the fulfillment of what Jesus meant by "Thy kingdom come, on earth as it is in heaven."

Remembering the Lord

Several places in the New Testament make reference to remembering the Lord when we gather together as the church. The word *remember* is a word that means more than just to recall or rethink. It can be taken literally as "re-assembly" or "re-construction." The central purpose of coming together as the body of Christ is to remind ourselves who is at the center of all things and, by extension, who we are as His people. In the Old Testament, the people of God did this by recounting over and over again the stories of God's redemptive miracles. This kind of remembrance can also be seen in Psalm 105 as well as here in Psalm 77:11–15:

> I will remember the works of the Lord; surely I will remember Your wonders of old. I will also meditate on all Your work, and talk of Your deeds. Your way, O God, is in the sanctuary; Who is so great a God as our God? You are the God who does wonders; You have declared Your strength among the peoples. You have with Your arm redeemed Your people, the sons of Jacob and Joseph. Selah.
>
> —NKJV

Jesus gathered with His disciples on the last night before His passion and instituted the Lord's Supper, also called communion. He gave it to them as they were gathered together with Him.

> And he took bread, and when he had given thanks, he broke it and gave it to them, saying, "This is my body, which is given for you. Do this in remembrance of me."
>
> —Luke 22:19

Paul recounted this event a few decades later to the church of Corinth with remarkable detail. It's important to remember that Paul was not one of the original apostles present that night. He stated emphatically that what he was sharing with them he received by supernatural revelation from Jesus Himself.

> For I received from the Lord what I also delivered to you, that the Lord Jesus on the night when he was betrayed took bread, and when he had given thanks, he broke it, and said, "This is my body, which is for you. Do this in remembrance of me."
> —1 CORINTHIANS 11:23–24

A few things stand out as significant. First of all, in both instances, the word *remembrance* is used. Jesus uses the physical symbol of the bread to illustrate His body. As He breaks it, He calls His followers to receive the bread and remember that, at the cross, His body was broken into pieces for our redemption.

On the other side of the cross and resurrection, where death was killed, we are called to gather and reassemble His body. This is what happens when we all come together around the resurrected Christ. We are literally bringing the broken members of His body, and it is there that the same Spirit that raised Christ from the dead breathes afresh upon us. (See Romans 8:11.)

During His earthly ministry, the anointing took residency upon Jesus, the unique One who was completely God and completely human. Since the outpouring of the Holy Spirit at Pentecost, the same anointing that fell upon the believers then now resides upon our present-day, many-membered body of Christ. Each member is significant yet incomplete without the other members. When this many-membered body comes together in unity of spirit, we are actually *remembering* Christ and demonstrating on Earth and to the spirit realm the supremacy of God's wisdom and victory.

Metrics of the Kingdom

Confession: I am always measuring things. As a pastor, I measure attendance, offerings, baptisms, and small-group participation. Most pastors are somewhat myopic when it comes to metrics and we shape what we do or don't do by what we see growing. Many times our decisions are determined more by spreadsheets than calloused knees. While I think it is good stewardship in the natural to pay attention to such things, we must be careful not to put too much stock in numbers. I have come to discover that God doesn't do math the way I do it. Addition isn't always a blessing, and subtraction isn't always a curse. When it comes to determining the health of a body of believers, more important than counting is weighing.

There is an account in the Old Testament of God's glorious presence invading a corporate gathering of His people with a radical result. Solomon had just finished the first temple and was dedicating it to the worship of Yahweh when His manifest presence filled it and overwhelmed everyone present.

> Now Solomon assembled the elders of Israel and all the heads of the tribes, the chief fathers of the children of Israel, in Jerusalem, that they might bring the ark of the covenant of the Lord up from the City of David, which is Zion. Therefore all the men of Israel assembled with the king at the feast, which was in the seventh month. So all the elders of Israel came, and the Levites took up the ark. Then they brought up the ark, the tabernacle of meeting, and all the holy furnishings that were in the tabernacle. The priests and the Levites brought them up. Also King Solomon, and all the congregation of Israel who were assembled with him before the ark, were sacrificing sheep and oxen that could not be counted or numbered for multitude. Then the priests brought in the ark of the covenant of the Lord to its place, into the inner sanctuary of the temple, to the Most Holy Place, under the wings of the cherubim. For the cherubim spread their wings over the place of the ark, and the cherubim overshadowed the ark and its poles. The poles extended so that the ends of the poles of the ark could be seen from the holy place, in front of the inner sanctuary; but they could not be seen from outside. And they are there to this day. Nothing was in the ark except the two tablets which Moses put there at Horeb, when the Lord made a covenant with the children of Israel, when they had come out of Egypt.
> And it came to pass when the priests came out of the Most Holy Place (for all the priests who were present had sanctified themselves, without keeping to their divisions), and the Levites who were the singers, all those of Asaph and Heman and Jeduthun, with their sons and their brethren, stood at the east end of the altar, clothed in white linen, having cymbals, stringed instruments and harps, and with them one hundred and twenty

priests sounding with trumpets — indeed it came to pass, when the trumpeters and singers were as one, to make one sound to be heard in praising and thanking the Lord, and when they lifted up their voice with the trumpets and cymbals and instruments of music, and praised the Lord, saying: "For He is good, for His mercy endures forever," that the house, the house of the Lord, was filled with a cloud, so that the priests could not continue ministering because of the cloud; for the glory of the Lord filled the house of God.

—2 Chronicles 5:2–14, nkjv

The Hebrew word for the glory of God is *kavod*, and it means "heavy." Its original, more concrete meaning is in reference to battle array, as in a shield or armament. The weightiness of God's manifest presence in the midst of His people caused their physical bodies to respond in complete surrender. This heaviness of His glory filled the temple in response to an environment appropriately ordered and filled with praise and worship. Imagine what it must have been like, after all of the preparation and training, to gather in this magnificent building, captivated by sensory overload at all of the sights, scents, and sounds. Then imagine seeing it all eclipsed by a supernatural invasion of the God of the universe, riding in on His glory cloud.

This is what I mean by weighing versus counting. It's possible to have a crowd but not an environment that is prepared and inviting to God's glory. If numbers are the measure of success, then the church is failing in comparison to sporting events and concerts being held in arenas. I know firsthand what it is like to stand up in front of thousands of people in a church sanctuary and feel nothing but indifference and distraction as the dominant spirits in the room. We should not expect God to invade such territory with His glory. God will not be mocked. When we gather with prepared hearts and godly reverence, desiring to honor Him with worship and adoration, we are in good company with those whose expectation and hunger become magnetic to the presence of God.

If we only evaluate or judge a church service by what is visible to the eyes and ears, then we stand in danger of being secular Christians, no different from the world. I believe this explains why you can walk into some worship services where worship songs are sung and messages are preached as in other places, yet the atmosphere is dead.

I have personally visited underground, illegal churches in Cuba that meet under blue tarps. I've sat on plastic lawn chairs and worshiped while their musicians have played on old and broken instruments. The pastors are poor and unknown, and the people are persecuted. In those settings that most Americans would find less than excellent, the anointing of God is manifested. Miracles take place, the tangible presence of God is felt, and the lost find eternal life.

In contrast, I have been in extraordinarily large worship venues with millions of dollars of lights and sound. I've walked out of some of those types of settings disappointed because there was no anointing.

Where there is no revelation that produces expectation, there is little anointing.

The corporate anointing becomes a collective revelation of God's glory present in our midst. In this atmosphere, there is laser focus upon the exalted Lord and His divine presence. Prayer, worship, and expectation are the ingredients that God is looking for. They are His invitation to show up.

> When the Day of Pentecost had fully come, they were all with one accord in one place. And suddenly there came a sound from heaven, as of a rushing mighty wind, and it filled the whole house where they were sitting. Then there appeared to them divided tongues, as of fire, and one sat upon each of them. And they were all filled with the Holy Spirit and began to speak with other tongues, as the Spirit gave them utterance.
>
> —ACTS 2:1–4, NKJV

This is what took place on the day of Pentecost, the birthday of the church, when God unleashed His Spirit upon His people. Every time His people gather in His name, praying and worshiping God in Spirit and truth, the dynamics of the anointing increase exponentially. There is so much more going on than meets the eye.

What would it look like for us to measure the success or effectiveness of our corporate gatherings by the degree of breakthrough that took place? Isaiah wrote and described the breakthrough power of the anointing:

And it shall come to pass in that day, that his burden shall be taken away from off thy shoulder, and his yoke from off thy neck, and the yoke shall be destroyed because of the anointing.

—Isaiah 10:27, kjv

I believe a greater revelation of this truth will change our worship gatherings as well as our understanding of the significance that each member plays. It will shift us from a "come and see" church to a "come and be" church. We can only pursue what we define, and we can only define what we understand. As long as we limit our understanding of the anointing to a personal or individual reality, we will see the corporate gatherings of the church as optional or, worse, unnecessary.

The Fullness of God's House

Just as we saw in the experience and encounter Jacob had with God, it's possible to be in the house of God and not experience the fullness. We may draw a measure of blessing and encouragement from gathering together with other believers, but we often leave on the table the more that God has for us. This is why we need a true covenant understanding, by way of revelation from the Spirit of God, of the deep riches found flowing in the river of God's corporate blessing, which is accessible through His church.

How precious is your lovingkindness, O God! Therefore the children of men put their trust under the shadow of Your wings. They are abundantly satisfied with the fullness of Your house, and You give them drink from the river of Your pleasures.

—Psalm 36:7–8, nkjv

In the next chapter, we are going to dig deeper into how the spiritual soil of God's house provides the perfect nutrients to shape, strengthen, and sustain us as the people of God living in the midst of a chaotic world.

Chapter Six
FLOURISH IN YOUR IDENTITY

Gabriel Nagy was a man who couldn't remember who he was. All he knew was that his car was wrecked, his head had been wounded, and he was wandering aimlessly, trying to find food, shelter, and someone to help him remember who he was. This was on January 21, 1987. Gabriel had suffered a traumatic brain injury producing a severe case of amnesia. He had forgotten who he was and ended up sleeping in the woods and then on the beach for months. Confused, he took odd jobs in construction and on fishing boats, wherever he could find work to earn some cash. To dull the pain and anxiety of not knowing truly who he was, he drank alcohol, all the while hoping that a miracle would happen. He desperately wanted his memory back so he could go home, wherever that was.[1]

After months and months of living in the middle of a nightmare, he met a man named Barry. Barry was a trucker turned pastor who saw something of value in him. Pastor Barry invited Gabriel to take shelter in his church and become its caretaker. It was in the welcoming environment of this little Australian church called River of Life that Gabriel's true identity began to return to him. Like little snapshots of a previous life, his real name began to reappear. Images of loved ones and a life he once lived reemerged. Years had gone by, and he had almost given up hope of ever recovering his true identity, but he was not the only one searching for him.

Ever since the day his car was found burned out on the side of the road, a police officer had been searching for him. Now, over twenty years later, in preparing for the final court proceedings that would declare Gabriel dead, Constable Robinson decided to take one more look. Around this same time, Gabriel had used his real name to apply for a Medicare card in order to receive a much-needed cataract surgery. When the investigating officer searched the system, a hit appeared with a location. Officer Robinson reached out to Gabriel, who had been living a life filled with holes and missing memories. But upon their meeting, the officer was able to answer Gabriel's question of who he really was.

Gabriel discovered that he had a wonderful life before his accident. On the day he went missing, he had called his wife and told her that he would be home for lunch. On his way home, driving along a rural road, he had some sort of an accident and suffered a severe head injury. The scar of that wound was still present on the back of his head some twenty-three years later. His wife and their young daughter had never given up hope that he was still alive, though they fought the fear that their husband and father was probably dead. Even when they moved further away to the Sunshine Coast in New Queensland, they kept their address available in the phone book, in case he would ever look for them.

After taking some time to process this news, Gabriel, with the help of the authorities, made one of the most anxiety-ridden phone calls of his life. Upon hearing the voice of his now adult daughter call him "daddy," the memories that had been hidden deep in his brain came rushing back to the surface, and the years of darkness were dispelled. He had finally been reintroduced to himself.

What You Don't Know

It's common in our culture to say, "What you don't know can't hurt you," but there isn't a more untrue statement. It's very often the things that we are ignorant of that have the most lethal effect upon our lives and, ultimately, our destinies. The prophet Hosea said it so powerfully: "My people are destroyed for lack of knowledge" (Hosea 4:6). As we can see from this scriptural truth, it is actually the realities we don't know or have an understanding of that have the potent power to destroy us. This is why having an understanding of our true identity in Christ is such an essential revelation for each of us to have. Without it, we stand a real probability of living our lives under an assumed identity, kept far away from the life we were originally created to live.

Oftentimes we imagine that issues of identity are problems people outside of the kingdom of God struggle with, but this is an unfortunate inaccuracy. Just because we have been saved by God's grace and born again by the Spirit of God does not guarantee an automatic and mature understanding of our brand-new identity in Christ.

There are countless numbers of believers who are living out a life of lack, isolation, and loneliness because they have believed a lie about who they are or aren't. Fortunately, Jesus not only came to save us from our sins but also to bring us truth that radically reshapes our understanding of who we are as well as *why* we are.

> Jesus said to those Jews who believed Him, "If you abide in My word, you are My disciples indeed. And you shall know the truth, and the truth shall make you free."
> —JOHN 8:31–32, NKJV

One of the strategies of hell, especially in this generation, is to bring confusion into our understanding of identity. Literally, we live in a world that is suffering from an identity crisis of epidemic proportion. It is manifesting itself in sexual identity dysphoria, political tribalism, and so many other unhealthy manifestations. We've become immune to them because they have taken root gradually. But if we were to go back in a time machine to thirty years ago, we would be shocked about where we are and how broken people's senses of identity are, yet we would see why so many lives are shattered.

Why is it even showing up in the church? As people are searching for answers to life's questions, many are turning to the church, hoping that God will bring them peace and a sense of satisfaction. If the message and culture inside the church isn't counterculture but culturally accommodating, it will become an incubator for unhealthy beliefs instead of a surgical ward that removes spiritually transmitted diseases such as wrong identity beliefs.

Shaped by Family

Perhaps the greatest influence on our sense of identity, or the lack thereof, is family. Our understanding of who we are is massively shaped by our grandparents, parents, and siblings. Without those voices in our lives, we either live isolated as orphans, merely surviving but not thriving, or we search out alternative structures to fill the hole within us.

As I look back over my life, like many of you, I recall moments that have defined who I am. Moments of hearing my grandma and grandpa talk about their lives and experiences. Looking through old photo albums and laughing at memories that we have all shared or heard countless times helped create a foundation of what it meant to be a Cummings. This is one of the reasons that God created family in the first place — as a secure, relational environment in which identity and history are transmitted and handed down as legacy from one generation to the next. It's interesting to notice that, from the very beginning, family was God's idea. It was the very first institution that God created. From it, every other institution (including the church) emerged. There is a reason for that.

So many young people are growing up without a sense of family. Divorce has ravaged our families and splintered what is supposed to be generational blessing into a thousand curses of insecurity. Kids have no idea where home truly is. They spend time in different homes and live in households with people who don't share the same last name. Polls and researchers are now discovering that many from the Millennial generation are placing close friends and nonblood relationships as higher priority than those with a biological connection.

I don't state this to condemn those who have gone through the pains of divorce or live in blended households. I lived in such a situation growing up, and my parents did a great job making our home secure. But we cannot ignore the toll that the breakdown of the nuclear family has taken on society as a whole, nor the impact it has had on our sense of identity.

The church is described as the household of God, of which we are all members after salvation. We were strangers and foreigners before Jesus, but all of that has changed. We are now family. God is our Father, and Jesus is our older brother. Each of us has been adopted and brought into the house, with a place designated for us at the table of the Lord.

> Now, therefore, you are no longer strangers and foreigners, but fellow citizens with the saints and members of the household of God, having been built upon the foundation of the apostles and prophets, Jesus Christ Himself being the chief cornerstone.
> —Ephesians 2:19–20, nkjv

Planting ourselves in a church, which is the family of God, is an essential aspect of discovering our true, eternal identity. It's the environment where we hear the Father speak His affirmation over us through those who serve as spiritual fathers, mothers, brothers, and sisters. In God's house, the spiritual foundations have framed a place for us to remember who we are by looking back at the story we were woven into even before we took our first breath. To live outside this environment doesn't change who we are, it just means living like the man who lost his memory, vaguely sensing that there is a life full of love out there waiting for us but held hostage to our lack of knowledge and experience. If we're going to flourish, we're going to do it together, in the Father's house.

Identity is the battlefield that the devil loves to use against those whom God anoints. Even Jesus Christ was not exempt from this challenge.

After thirty-plus years of living in preparation and obscurity, Jesus stepped onto the scene of history in a dramatic fashion. John was baptizing people in the Jordan unto repentance, preparing the way for the Messiah to emerge. This is likely the same location of the Jordan where Joshua led the children of Israel across into the Promised Land to possess their inheritance. It is only appropriate that it was here that John was calling the people of God to remember who they were and calling them back to faithfulness to their covenant. It is also appropriate that here we see the new Joshua—Jesus—step into the waters of the Jordan to set God's people free from wandering in the wilderness and leading them into the Promised Land.

Instead of opening up the Jordan for them to walk through as Joshua had done, God the Father ripped open the heavens and spoke over His Son, Jesus.

> When He had been baptized, Jesus came up immediately from the water; and behold the heavens were opened to Him, and He saw the Spirit of God descending like a dove and alighting upon Him. And suddenly a voice came from heaven, saying "This is My beloved Son, in whom I am well pleased."
> —MATTHEW 3:16–17, NKJV

What an affirming moment for a son. I am sure that throughout Jesus's life, God was at work, revealing to Jesus who He was and what was His mission. This moment must've been a capstone moment for Him and a public revelation for the world.

Immediately, Jesus went into the wilderness to be tempted for forty days and nights. The devil waited until Jesus was at His weakest before making His appearance, but when he does, he goes straight for the jugular and attacks his identity.

> Now when the tempter came to Him, he said, "If you are the Son of God, command that these stones become bread."
> —MATTHEW 4:3, NKJV

I remember reading this and thinking to myself, *How in the world could the devil be so dumb? God the Father had just spoken over Jesus in such a powerful way by calling Him His Son and saying that He was pleased with Him. Why would the enemy dare challenge Christ's identity and not something else?*

As soon as I thought this, I heard the Holy Spirit whisper to me that identity is a headpin in all of us. In bowling, a headpin is the center pin at the front of the other nine. If you strike the headpin just right, it will cause a ricochet effect to knock over the rest (called a strike). In the same way, if the enemy can destroy or distort our sense of identity, all the other issues fall like scattered bowling pins. We can be dominated if we can be denominated or have our identity divided.

This was even true of Jesus in His humanity. The devil knew that a false sense of identity was a human vulnerability, and he aimed his attack at Jesus in this arena. His goal was to cause Jesus to be insecure about who He was. Insecurity causes us to make decisions from the wrong source of motivation. Jesus had nothing to prove.

If the devil would dare attack Jesus's sense of identity, what are the odds that he has left it off the table in his war against your destiny? If Jesus, with an audible announcement from the Father, was subject to temptation, how much more must we shore up our understanding and gain a solid revelation of our identity in Christ? Remember where Jesus was when the Father spoke to Him about who He was? It was while He was in the midst of the covenant community of Israel, standing knee-deep in the waters of the Jordan that His Father had announced to heaven, hell, and all of creation who Jesus was. Now He was able to endure privately the attacks against His identity because of what He received from the Father corporately.

A New Passport Issued

When anyone comes into a relationship with God through Jesus Christ, there is a metamorphosis that takes place in the spirit that is invisible to the naked eye. Not only are our sins forgiven, but a new nature is given to us at the moment of conversion. The old Adamic nature that we were born with is eclipsed by the indwelling Holy Spirit, awakening our spiritually dead souls and grafting into our new spirit the DNA of our heavenly Father. In that moment, we literally become a *new creation*. Paul states this so clearly in 2 Corinthians 5:17–18:

> Therefore if anyone is in Christ, he is a new creation; old things have passed away; behold, all things have become new. Now all things are of God, who has reconciled us to Himself through Jesus Christ, and has given us the ministry of reconciliation.
> —NKJV

A new heart, a new nature, and a new identity in Christ are granted. Along with this new identity comes the issuing of a new spiritual passport with all of the privileges that come with the citizenship of heaven. Maybe you have never thought about it that way, but consider this for a moment: when you are a citizen of any given nation and you want to leave your country to travel to another, you are issued a passport. If you've ever gone on a short-term mission trip or traveled outside your country, you know what I am talking about. After you have verified that you were born in a particular nation and met the requirements for proof of citizenship, the government issues you a passport confirming that you live under their jurisdiction and therefore are subject to the full rights and benefits of said nation.

Spiritually speaking, all of us are born into this world with a passport identifying us as part of the sinful nation of Adam. This places us under the curse, binds us as slaves to sin, and reveals our guilt and sentence to hell and death. Because of our Adamic national identity, we are enemies of God and His kingdom. It's a hopeless place to be in because, in our own strength, there is no possible way to change this identity. But through Christ, we can change our national allegiance and join the kingdom of God.

The gospel is good news because it tells the story of God's becoming one of us, entering behind enemy lines and making it possible for the children of Adam to become children of God. We exodus from the broken, dark, sinful reality of our old nature, accept the invitation to be born again into God's kingdom, and receive brand new passports. The new passports don't have any indication at all of our old allegiances, and in God's new family, there are no second-class citizens.

> And you were dead in the trespasses and sins in which you once walked, following the course of this world, following the prince of the power of the air, the spirit that is now at work in the sons of disobedience—among whom we all once lived in the passions of our flesh, carrying out the desires of the body and the mind, and were by nature children of wrath, like the rest of mankind. But God, being rich in mercy, because of the great love with which he loved us, even when we were dead in our trespasses, made us alive together with Christ—by grace you have been saved—and raised us up with him and seated us with him in the heavenly places in Christ Jesus, so that in the coming ages he might show the immeasurable riches of his grace in kindness toward us in Christ Jesus. For by grace you have been saved through faith. And this is not your own doing; it is the gift of God, not a result of works, so that no one may boast. For we are his workmanship, created in Christ Jesus for good works, which God prepared beforehand, that we should walk in them.
> Therefore remember that at one time you Gentiles in the flesh, called "the uncircumcision" by what is called the circumcision, which is made in the flesh by hands—remember that you were at that time separated from Christ, alienated from the commonwealth of Israel and strangers to the covenants of promise, having no hope and without God in the world. But now in Christ Jesus you who once were far off have been brought near by the blood of Christ.
> —Ephesians 2:1–13

The Bible is explicit about how God sees our new identity in Christ as opposed to who we were before believing the gospel. There is such a dramatic contrast found in this section of Ephesians. In Adam we were:

1. Dead in sin

2. Influenced by Satan

3. Swept into the current of the world

4. Driven by our appetites and lusts

5. Children of wrath

6. Separated from Christ

7. Outsiders from God

8. Alienated from covenant promises

9. Hopeless

10. Godless

But after being born again and brought into the family of God, everything changes. We are now:

1. Alive in Christ

2. Raised up and seated in heavenly places

3. Objects of God's grace and kindness

4. God's workmanship

5. Called to good works and purposes

6. Close to God

7. At peace with God

8. Eternally alive

9. Citizens of the kingdom of God

10. Family members of God's royal household

What an amazing transformation that takes place in a person's life when Christ comes into it. Everything changes in ways that aren't immediately evident or obvious. Some of us still look the same on the outside, but for all of us our inside world has shifted from darkness to light and death to life in a moment.

This new passport that we have in Christ gives us access to all of the covenant promises in God's Word. We no longer have to live under the dominion of sin and Satan, because we have been translated from one kingdom into another.

> He has delivered us from the domain of darkness and transferred us to the kingdom of his beloved Son, in whom we have redemption, the forgiveness of sins.
>
> —COLOSSIANS 1:13–14

Thieves of Your New Identity

What I find so disturbing—especially as a pastor—is watching men and women, who I know have a new destiny to fulfill in Christ, live far below their new birthright. Even though Jesus has become their Lord and Savior, they have not yet realized the scope and significance of the change that has shifted their eternal destiny and identity. The devil has convinced them that they are exactly the way that they were before and that nothing has changed.

He has pulled a blinder over the eyes of their heart to keep them from realizing how different their lives can be and how different they are destined to be now that they are no longer under the curse of Adam.

Bad theology

There is so much bad theology that plagues the church today. I have seen some of the worst of it on bumper stickers plastered on believers' cars. For example, one bumper sticker said, "Christians aren't perfect; we're just forgiven." While we are forgiven, being a Christian is so much more than this. I've heard people state emphatically and even sing it in gospel songs that they are just "old sinners saved by grace."

The truth is you *were* a sinner, but as soon as you reached for Christ and were born again, you ceased being a sinner anymore. You are now a saint. That doesn't mean you no longer will commit sins; it just means it is no longer your identity or nature.

> And such were some of you. But you were washed, but you were sanctified, but you were justified in the name of the Lord Jesus and by the Spirit of our God.
>
> —1 CORINTHIANS 6:11, NKJV

Why is this such a problem? Because we live up to what we believe we are destined for. If you see yourself as a sinner, then sin will become or remain your normal. If you see yourself as washed, cleansed, and full of power to overcome, you will resist sin and temptation. If you see yourself as a slave, you will take orders. If you see yourself as royalty, you will see temptation as below you and a trap to thwart your calling. The devil very often uses demonic tools and trickery to steal the power of our true identities from us. If he can steal truth, he can plant the lie that deceives, detonates, and destroys us from the inside out.

The four Cs: comparison, complacency, competition, and compromise

Comparison will steal the beauty of your testimony and uniqueness of God's design by causing you to measure your value and progress through the metric of others. Complacency will convince you that you're all right where you are and zap the zeal to draw closer to God. Competition, a cousin to comparison, seeks to derail your destiny by directing your passion and energy toward others, off-ramping you from the process of progress, leaving you stranded in a parking ramp of bitterness.

Perhaps the greatest identity thief is compromise. If the enemy can't get you to turn your back on Jesus or offer you a sweeter substitute, he will try to get you to compromise. The story of Nehemiah provides a textbook example of this tactic.

While making amazing progress toward rebuilding the walls to secure the city of Jerusalem, Nehemiah was invited to meet with those who had worked overtime to ensure that his task would never be completed. Sanballat, Tobiah, and their cronies used intimidation, violence, and every other tool in their arsenal, but nothing had been able to stop the supernatural results under Nehemiah's excellent leadership.

One day, a messenger approaches with a proposition for him:

> Sanballat and Geshem sent to me, saying, "Come and let us meet together at Hakkephirim in the plain of Ono." But they intended to do me harm. And I sent a messenger to them, saying, "I am doing a great work and I cannot come down. Why should the work stop while I leave and come down to you?"
> —NEHEMIAH 6:2–3

Beware of anyone calling to meet you in the valley of "Oh-No." This was a call to negotiate. When the devil cannot get you to sell out, he will often get you to settle or make a deal. Nehemiah realized the harm that this would mean to himself but also to the lives and futures of those who were working with him. He recognized that all the hard work was actually a "great work."

We need a similar revelation. When we feel challenged in our identity, we can never compromise. We can't allow the devil to get us off the wall, where God is building a life inside us shaped like Jesus. We can't concede territory in any part of our identity—not in our past, present, or future.

The Over and Under of Church

Strength comes by doing the right things in the right place with the right people. Consider the gym. I have had seasons where I spent a lot of time at the gym, working to lose weight and get in shape. When I have dedicated myself to the process, I have been amazed at the results. When I have neglected the gym because of busyness or just plain laziness, I have watched my strength dissipate. In my mind, I know I should go. I even know the routines and the steps necessary to achieve the results I want. But it takes more than just paying monthly dues or reading blogs about fitness. You have to go to the gym and use the equipment to get strong.

In much the same way, the church is our spiritual gym. We need the environment that has all the things our souls need to grow and get in shape. Can you be a Christian without being plugged into a local church? Yes. Can you be a healthy, flourishing Christian without being planted in a thriving local church? Probably not. Is it because there is a deficit in our salvation? No. It's because the way God has designed us, and the body of Christ requires us to live according to the *law of over and under* in regards to others and ourselves. Let me explain.

The over

In ourselves—the fallen human beings we are—we have an amazing confidence in ourselves as individuals almost to a fault. This can be a dangerous error in our faith journey that can leave us lacking. Paul, writing to the church at Rome, reminded them of this overconfidence:

For by the grace given to me I say to everyone among you not
to think of himself more highly than he ought to think, but to
think with sober judgment, each according to the measure of
faith that God has assigned. For as in one body we have many
members, and the members do not all have the same function,
so we, though many, are one body in Christ, and individually
members one of another.

—Romans 12:3–4

When Paul admonishes us not to think more highly about ourselves
than we ought to, he contrasts that with "sober judgment." The opposite
of sober is intoxicated. Sometimes our view of our own abilities and giftedness is the equivalent of being drunk. When you're under the influence
of alcohol, it impairs your speech and affects your ability to walk straight.
The key to not looking foolish because of overconfidence is realizing we
are only one part of what God is doing. We are a significant part, but not
the whole. We have an assignment and a destiny, but ours are interwoven
with those of others. Ours are not stand-alone destinies. We have a stand-
together calling in Jesus.

You are gifted, but you are not complete. You need other gifts to
strengthen your gifts. Just like in a gym, you have someone to spot you as
you reach for new *personal* bests. Likewise, the church is not an environment to compete with others. It's an environment in which we complete
one another. We need to get over ourselves and get under authority!

The under

If living overconfidently is dangerous, then the opposite is also true.
Underestimating our own significance to the kingdom of God is equally
detrimental to our flourishing in God. The devil is a master manipulator
and discourager. He works hard at wearing us out with the lies that our
life doesn't matter, that we are on the outside, and that we are lucky to just
be going to heaven. Any ideas or dreams we may have about living lives
of significance and changing the world around us are dismissed as pipe
dreams or something that we don't deserve. We so easily forget everything
that we have in the kingdom of God is undeserved and unmerited. That's
why it's called "grace." The Passion translation says it best:

You are the body of the Anointed One, and each of you is a unique and vital part of it.

—1 Corinthians 12:27, tpt

It's difficult for us to see beyond our fears of insignificance or perhaps our past failures that haunt us. We look in the mirror and see all the reasons why we are overlooked, underestimated, and left behind. But if we could see through the lens of the kingdom of God, we would see ourselves the way the Father does. You would realize that you are far more important than you believe. Instead of your past disqualifying you, you'll see how it actually served to shape you. Instead of God condemning you for it, you'll see how He is the master artist who takes the raw edges of our lives and weaves them together into a masterful tapestry of grace.

Made for This

When I was a kid, I watched old reruns of a show called *The Addams Family*, a comedy about a houseful of monster-like, creepy family members living in the middle of suburbia. One of the characters in the show was called "Thing." Thing was a detached hand that lived in a box. It would crawl out like a spider to answer the phone or fetch a glass of water. Watching guests' eyes pop out of their head every time Thing came out of the box was hilarious. It was also very creepy, because it was unnatural. A hand isn't supposed to walk around by itself. It's meant to be attached to an arm, that is attached to a shoulder, that is attached to a torso, with legs, feet, and ultimately a head.

In the same way, a Christian is meant to be a part of a body. We don't notice a hand until it is presented in a way that is out of context. Our lives only make sense in the context of the local church. Christians were not meant to be walking around like stray pieces of a Mr. Potato Head set. We need a body to be connected. We need *others*. Why? Because the God we worship is Lord over an eternal community of love and we were created in His image. We thrive and flourish as members of Christ's body when we are walking and pursuing God together.

Chapter Seven
FLOURISH IN COMMUNITY

I have had the privilege of traveling to many nations to minister the gospel and strengthen churches and leaders. Places like India have become very near and dear to my heart because of the relationships Jane and I have developed with our dear friends that lead this nation. We have made several trips there, traveled to its remotest corners, and invested hundreds of thousands of dollars into building schools and orphanages. But there are other places I do not know so well.

The other day someone asked me if I had ever been to England. I had to pause and think about it for a moment. Technically, I have been to England, meaning I have stood on English soil. If you were to track me with a GPS, there would be a record of my physical presence on the island nation, but have I *been* to England? I ended up answering the question this way: "Well, I've been in the Heathrow Airport on a layover, but I've never seen or experienced England for real."

I think there are a lot of Christians who have been in church but have not really experienced church the way God intended. We may have gone to church, sat through the services, and even attended regularly on a once-a-week schedule, only to be left wanting and asking the question, "Is this all there is to this church thing?"

In order to really begin to flourish in the courts of our God, we are going to have to leave the terminal of spectatorship and pass beyond the secured barriers of an isolated life. We're going to have to leave the airport, so to speak, and travel up and down the streets of the city, interacting with people in their native environments and unpacking our bags. As long as we view church as a place we spend time occasionally on our way someplace else, we will miss out on one of the very things we need in order to flourish and thrive in the kingdom of God—community.

What Is Community?

Webster's Dictionary defines *community* as "a unified body of individuals...people with common interests living in a particular area." The word itself is a combination of "com," which means "together" and "une" which is "one or singular." So etymologically speaking, the word community means "together as one."[1]

This definition is supported by Scripture and gives a clearer description of how the body of Christ organically functions. We can also see how it describes the need for connectivity that every Christian has as part of their spiritual heritage and make up. We were created by community (a triune God) for community. The very story of God's creating mankind in the garden is also the first reference to community.

> Then God said, "Let us make man in our image, after our likeness."
>
> —GENESIS 1:26

The Godhead—Father, Son, and Holy Spirit—has dwelt as an eternal community within themselves. It was out of their "together as one," or as theologians have described it, "Trinity or tri-unity," that God created mankind and intrinsically coded community into our very nature. This is what it means in part to be made in the image of God. Out of everything God did create and described as "good" or "perfect," the only thing that was not good was the fact that man was alone. Woman was God's answer to Adam's lack of community. Instead of making her separately, God fashioned her from his side; thus, they were "one flesh."

In the church, God has performed another creative miracle by taking people from different backgrounds, causing each of us to drink of the same Spirit, and baptizing or immersing us all into one body—Christ's. This unifying act is more than an ethereal picture of our ideological unity; it is a spiritual reality that has material and practical implications. We were made for unity because, alone, we are not complete. What we need in order to flourish and fulfill our assigned destiny is not only found in a vertical relationship with God the Father, Son, and Holy Spirit. We also need the horizontal community of one another to strengthen and add to what is incomplete in ourselves and our faith. This is biblical Christianity. Until we have allowed ourselves to truly be planted into the fertile soil of human community, we have not truly experienced life in the kingdom of God. We may be in close proximity to it, we may have been *to* church, but we have not truly experienced what it means to *be the church.*

Living Stones

I grew up in the Great Lakes state of Michigan. Minus two years of living in Kansas City, Missouri, I have lived here and pastored here to this day. Some of my favorite memories of growing up here are of the long road trips in the backseat of my grandparents' van when we would drive to places "up north" (what we Michiganders call the remote area of upper Michigan).

One of the unique things that always fascinated me was the fieldstone homes that are scattered all over the rural parts of the state. When I would point them out, my grandmother would tell me about the home she was born in that was also a "stone home." These peculiar homes were made by farmers as they cleaned their land of stones or carried larger rocks out of the river bed near their plot of land. Even to this day, when I see one of these houses, I can't keep myself from staring, because each of these beautifully crafted homes are as unique as the stones that make them up.

The church and the community that flows from it are like these peculiar homes. Peter calls believers "living stones" whom God is using to build a spiritual dwelling place for His presence.

> As you come to him, a living stone rejected by men but in the sight of God chosen and precious, you yourselves like living stones are being built up as a spiritual house, to be a holy priesthood, to offer spiritual sacrifices acceptable to God through Jesus Christ. For it stands in Scripture: "Behold, I am laying in Zion a stone, a cornerstone chosen and precious, and whoever believes in him will not be put to shame."
> —1 PETER 2:4–6

God sees each of us as chosen and precious, living stones. The house or community that God is building is measured by the true Cornerstone, Jesus, who was rejected and cast away because He didn't measure up to the standards and expectations of the religious spirit dominant in His day. Jesus was the stone *that the builders rejected*. (See Psalm 118:22; Matthew 21:42.)

When a farmer builds one of these homes, he doesn't use hand-cut stones or man-made bricks. Instead, He finds unique stones that have been exposed to the elements over time, baked in the heat of summer, and shaped by the fierce currents of rivers. A true artisan has the eye to know where to place them to perfectly fit together on the wall alongside the other stones. This is also the way God builds His house.

Our lives are shaped by our unique stories, trials, and experiences, like the elements that form those stones. No two people in the body of Christ have made the same odyssey into the kingdom, but our new lives in Christ tell the same story of God's amazing grace. The very things we feared would destroy us have been redeemed in Christ and now demonstrate the contour of His craftsmanship, as He perfectly places us into Him and next to each other.

On the other hand, the Babylonian system of this world wants to build with bricks and not stones. Bricks are artificial and intentionally uniform. They are lifeless stones, indistinguishable from one another and, in the end, disposable. The devil wants to steal the uniqueness from God's creation. He builds his counterkingdom by forcing people into the molds of conformity and shame. Instead of living stones where each tells a part of a greater story, he uses dead, nameless souls, shaped by hopelessness and imprisoned in the search for significance. This is how man in his best attempt started building his own society with himself at the center.

> "Come, let us make bricks, and burn them thoroughly." And they had bricks for stone, and bitumen for mortar. Then they said, "Come let us build ourselves a city and a tower with its top in the heavens, and let us make a name for ourselves."
> —Genesis 11:3–4

When God builds a house, He doesn't start with making bricks but by searching for stones—living stones. Each stone is masterfully inspected and placed in exactly the right position by the Builder. Only He has the eye to know where each stone fits. What may look like a pile of unimportant stones is built up row by row until it becomes a master crafted home in which God's wisdom is revealed. Every one of those stones finds its reason on the wall, next to the other. In the church, every individual finds their purpose and place in what God is building as His kingdom community.

The Prototype Community

When we think about the church as a local community, all kinds of things enter our minds. For me, my first mental image is the little church in Clarkston, Michigan, that I attended with my family as a young child. I can still smell the musty basement and taste the rusty water from the drinking fountain, which was flanked by a stack of Dixie cups. I can hear the squeaky wood theatre seats and visualize the pulpit as well as the after-church potlucks in the basement.

What do you imagine when you think of "church"? Whatever it is you see in your mind's eye becomes an icon of how you see the church as a community.

The prototype I constantly go back to as a pastor is the Book of Acts. I have no misconceptions that the church in the Book of Acts was perfect or even ideal. There were some pretty messy issues and arguments found in those twenty-eight chapters. But what also can be found from the very beginning of the Jesus movement among His followers was supernatural community.

> And with many other words he bore witness and continued to exhort them, saying, "Save yourselves from this crooked generation." So those who received his word were baptized, and there were added that day about three thousand souls.
> And they devoted themselves to the apostles' teaching and the fellowship, to the breaking of bread and the prayers. And awe came upon every soul, and many wonders and signs were being done through the apostles. And all who believed were together and had all things in common. And they were selling their possessions and belongings and distributing the proceeds to all, as any had need. And day by day, attending the temple together and breaking bread in their homes, they received their food with glad and generous hearts, praising God and having favor with all the people. And the Lord added to their number day by day those who were being saved.
> —ACTS 2:40–47

This description of the church is ground zero for how the culture of heaven was established from the very beginning—in community. There were thousands of new believers right from the start, as well as a few hundred who were leaders. There was an outpouring of supernatural generosity and a sense of awe at what God was doing in their midst. There was serious numeric growth taking place on a daily basis. You could safely describe what was taking place as a "revival" or "awakening."

From this epicenter of the outpoured Holy Spirit, the church moved out toward the uttermost parts of the Roman Empire and the world. As they went, they preached the gospel, demonstrated the presence of the kingdom of God in powerful signs and wonders, led people to Christ, and then established communities of believers called *ekklesia* or churches.[2]

Just as God knows that humans thrive best in households of families with mothers, fathers, and siblings, the church is an extension of this truth. Christians need other Christians in order to flourish. We are not designed to be closed systems. We are wired for community. One of the most significant words in these verses is the word *fellowship*.

This word *fellowship* in the original Greek is the word *koinonia*, which means "partnership or mutual participation in some project or event."[3] This is how Luke, when trying to articulate God's formation of the church, described their behavior. They all became partners together in the cause of the gospel and met together regularly to worship, pray, and commune in unity.

Before there were physical buildings called churches, there were core values that shaped the formation of Christ's body of believers. It was built with heavenly materials, living stones, held together by the Holy Spirit and all carrying the weight of God's glory in their midst. The church was a statement to a broken system of what God was building on the earth. Jesus did not come to start a religion that individuals could practice on their own, or that could be added on as an accessory to our private lives. Jesus came to be your personal Savior, not your private one. We were meant to do life with others, in unity.

Connected but Not Committed

In our individualistic American culture, we are connected to almost everything but committed to very little. Because we have choices and access to information and opportunities, it gives the illusion we don't really need church or community. After all, we can listen to a podcast, read a book, or worship in our cars without being a part of a local church.

It's usually not until we find ourselves in crisis or lonely that we realize how important the community of believers truly is. When something in our life is broken or suffering, that is when we look for help. In those moments, we need more than the monologue of a podcast or simulcast; we need the dialogue of other disciples.

While technology is wonderful and weekends hold many awesome options to spend our time, we make a grave spiritual error if we discount the significance that comes from faithfully being committed to a vision and a people. There is something in the environment of "church" that can't be replicated elsewhere.

I would even say there are ingredients God has spiritually built into the fellowship of believers that are necessary for every Christian to flourish in life. These gifts and tools are not found in any other worldly institution like they are in the church. It's far too easy to live in our Western civilization bubble and believe the lie that church is optional or outdated. Why do we need community in order to flourish? Because it is God's kingdom order. A spiritual family with whom we grow, pray, worship, and serve together is an invaluable source of strength that each of us need, whether we know it or not.

Locked within this Acts 2 pattern of the church as a living, breathing community are some distinct relationships each of us need in order to truly draw from the life-giving strength of this kingdom community and culture.

We Need Leaders to Speak into Our Lives

God has given the gift of leadership to the church in order to bring us to a place of maturity, just as He has given mothers, fathers, and older siblings to the family. There is an indispensable deposit a leader makes into a life that cannot be substituted (more about these leadership roles in the next chapter). When a leader invests into a developing leader, they are giving access to a life of wisdom and experience. Literally, their ceiling becomes our floor, as we won't have to repeat the mistakes they made.

As I look back on my journey as a leader, I am fully aware of the investment others made into me. They came in during the multiple tipping points in my life with words of confidence and affirmation that helped forge my character, correct areas of weakness, and infuse the courage I needed to believe I was able to do more than I ever imagined.

The Bible has so much to say about leadership, directly and indirectly. Look closely at and learn from the stories in the Old and New Testaments that serve as examples of good leadership and the ramifications of poor or missing leadership. It is vital that we recognize the role of leaders and our response to leadership in our lives.

> Having then gifts differing according to the grace that is given to us, let us use them: if prophecy, let us prophesy in proportion to our faith; or ministry, let us use it in our ministering; he who teaches, in teaching; he who exhorts, in exhortation; he who gives, with liberality; he who leads, with diligence.
>
> —ROMANS 12:6–8, NKJV

> Remember those who rule over you, who have spoken the word of God to you, whose faith follow, considering the outcome of their conduct.
>
> —HEBREWS 13:7, NKJV

The church is a nuclear reactor of kingdom potency, but without the voice of leaders, it can suffer Chernobyl-scale catastrophe. Unfortunately, in our attempt to be accepted by the world, the church has been vulnerable to adopt a worldly philosophy of leadership. This has led to corruption, isolation, and disappointment that has turned the hearts of many people away from finding their place of belonging in the community of faith. The way that Jesus dealt with how leaders are to function is, in many ways, the opposite of how the world operates.

> But Jesus called them to Himself and said, "You know that the rulers of the Gentiles lord it over them, and those who are great exercise authority over them. Yet it shall not be so among you; but whoever desires to become great among you, let him be your servant."
>
> —MATTHEW 20:25–26, NKJV

Right from the beginning, we see leaders such as the apostles and those whom they appointed as leaders of the people, who began to teach, shepherd, and oversee the growing body of believers. Even though our sinful nature has a tendency to resist leaders in our lives, it is imperative that we embrace the influence of others, not as a restriction, but as gifts from the Lord.

We Need Friends with Whom We Do Life

Close friendships are built around similar values and experiences. One of the greatest gifts God gives us is the gift of friendship. Often, we view church as an event that we attend instead of a community to which we belong. When we only see church as a place we go to once a week and our real friendships are rooted in other things, we miss out on what it means to truly have *koinonia* or fellowship.

When we prioritize building friendships within the community of the church, we not only become strengthened in our faith, but we also form bonds that will last a lifetime and beyond. Whether it is serving side by side with others or joining a small group or Bible study, we become knit together in the Spirit. Researchers have discovered an alarming reality that if someone doesn't develop at least one strong friendship in church, within a few months they will stop attending.

This is partly the fault of church-growth models we have bought into. We focus so much of our time and attention on getting people to show up for services or events that we have missed the glue that actually makes people want to be there—*each other.*

Fifty-nine times in the New Testament, the phrase *one another* is used to describe how we are to interact as fellow members of the household of God. Some of those instructions are for dealing with difficulties. The rest of them are reminders of how badly we need one another and how much benefit we give to one another when we are intentional about building friendships. My own experience bears this out.

When I was twelve years old, I received Jesus as my Savior while spending the summer with my grandparents. I had had a dramatic encounter with the Lord that forever marked me as called into the ministry. When I returned home to start school, I found myself a bit overwhelmed with the idea of going to church by myself. My parents believed in God but were not attending church at this time. They said it was fine if I wanted to attend, but I would have to find a ride.

I had a friend named Nate whose family was deeply involved at their church. Nate and I met on the soccer field in fourth grade and did not like one another very much at first. After a while, we became close friends until sixth grade when I moved away to a different school district across town. I had visited his youth group with him a few times, so I decided to reach out to him and see if I could begin going again with him and his family.

That decision marked a significant shift in my life and future. I attended First Assembly all the way through high school with Nate. We became deeply involved in the youth ministry, where a mini revival was taking place during our senior year of high school. We encountered the Lord in ways that marked us forever. We went on missions trips together, prayed together, worshipped together, and ate our youth pastor's ice cream without him knowing together. We even made up a nickname for ourselves centered on our make-believe basketball skills. We were the Atlas Brothers (a rip-off of the Globetrotters).

Now Nate lives in Minneapolis, and I live in Kalamazoo, but we are still close, covenant friends. Our wives are friends as well. We both lead large ministries and preach at each other's churches yearly. We share a bond in the Spirit that has been a source of strength and encouragement throughout the best and worst of times.

We all need friendships like this that keep us close to God and focused on His purpose for our lives. If it wasn't for the church, Nate and I would not be the friends or pastors we are today.

We Need Those to Whom We Bring Life

For every Timothy, there is a Paul. For every follower of Jesus, we must realize we are called to make disciples. It's easy to become self-focused and only think about our own needs and inadequacies, but we were created not only with a need to receive but also a call to give to others. We often get caught up into asking, "What's in it for me?" but fail to ask the better question, "What's in me for others?"

When we read the Book of Acts carefully, we see that the apostles picked up the same pattern Jesus demonstrated with them. They had followed the

Master for over three years, preparing for ministry. Then they were carrying out the Great Commission Jesus left them, part of which was to make disciples of others.

> Go therefore and make disciples of all nations, baptizing them in the name of the Father and of the Son and of the Holy Spirit, teaching them to observe all that I have commanded you.
> —MATTHEW 28:19, NKJV

> And the word of God continued to increase, and the number of the disciples multiplied greatly in Jerusalem, and a great many of the priests became obedient to the faith.
> —ACTS 6:7

You many not feel like it, but what is on the inside of you has the power to bring life to others. Your victories from yesterday can be someone's game plan for tomorrow. Most people think they are not far enough down the road of spiritual maturity to witness to others or be a mentor. This is a tactic of the devil to keep the church paralyzed and immobile. You may not be as mature as you want to be, or you may wish you knew more about the Bible or the Holy Spirit, but I promise you, there is someone who is a few steps behind you that needs your investment. Your iron can sharpen theirs (Proverbs 27:17). The key is not to attain to some spiritual status before God can use you to encourage someone else in their journey. The master key is to give what you have and God will give you more.

> "Follow my example, as I follow the example of Christ."
> —1 CORINTHIANS 11:1, NIV

> Freely you have received; freely give.
> —MATTHEW 10:8, NIV

We Need Difficult People Whom God Uses to Refine Our lives

If you find yourself evaluating the significance of church through the lens of fear, pain, or a cautionary attitude because of encounters that you have had with difficult people, you are not alone. So many people who love the Lord have given up on the church and chosen not to put roots down or to belong.

I remember my pastor saying one time, "The church is like Noah's Ark. It might stink at times, but it's the safest place to be."

As long as there are people involved, there is going to be conflict and injury. The larger a church gets, the odds of encountering difficult people or experiencing conflict increase exponentially. If we set the bar so high that church must be a perfect environment with perfect people before we decide to get rooted and grounded in community, we will forever have shallow root systems and fail to flourish. It's been said, "If you find the perfect church, don't go to it, because the moment you join it, it ceases to be perfect."

I don't believe we should be looking for a perfect church, but we should graft ourselves willingly into the *perfecting* church. God's goal and end game for a church are not to finally get all the bad people out and quarantine the good people. There are no good people. If you have a pulse, you have issues, period. So did God miss it? Are we more messed up than we realized, and therefore the church is no longer an instrument capable of bringing believers into maturity? Or is that exactly what God had in mind all along?

I believe God intentionally places difficult people in our lives at church. I also believe that God deals with difficult issues on the inside of us, utilizing the tools of conflict and differences with others. Where else do we learn how to forgive one another? How else can we model to the world the ministry of reconciliation if we can't do it in the family of God?

God is far more concerned with our conformity to Christ than He is with our comfort in this world. He is a master craftsman and one of His favorite chisels is conflict with others. We learn the greatest lessons about God's grace toward us when we are put into a position to love others when they least deserve it.

What a testimony the church can be (and often is) as we worship the same Lord in the same Holy Spirit with brothers and sisters of different ethnicities, political persuasions, economic levels, and personal preferences. The world can't get along, but they don't have the Spirit of God dwelling in them. Relational difficulties should not be a reason for us to avoid church. Instead, it's actually an opportunity to be the church before the world.

Chapter Eight
FLOURISH IN YOUR DESTINY

Let me begin by saying how much I love America. I was born here and have lived here all of my life. It is my home. I have also traveled all over the world, and I can honestly say that there is no other nation on the face of the earth I would rather live. I love all of our conveniences, creativity, and culture, and to be completely transparent, I rock the red, white, and blue every four years when the Olympic Games are televised. I am proud to be an American.

But there are some things that are challenging about this culture if you are going to actively pursue following Jesus Christ. Distinguishing the American culture from the kingdom culture at times requires us to see beyond the blurry boundary lines and repent of attitudes and assumptions that could hinder us and keep us from fulfilling our destiny in Christ.

One such issue that Christians living in a democracy have to wrestle with is the subject of authority. At the core of our American consciousness is a skepticism and disdain for anyone who would want to exert authority over us. Our entire foundation as a nation and people is rooted in what we call revolution. Another word for it is *rebellion* (right about now is when the hackles start going up on our patriotic backs). We vote leaders in, and we vote them out depending upon how we view them and their policies, principles, and performance. Rebellion against the system may be politically virtuous in some cases, but when it comes to how we relate to spiritual authority, it is dangerous to our soul.

While democracy may be the best form of human government that civilization has come up with, it is still flawed. When democracy is applied to the church and the way it is governed, it can be disastrous. The church is not part of the world's system and isn't meant to be governed after a carbon-copied way of the world. It is an embassy of heaven on Earth. Its government is not a democracy, but a monarchy under Jesus our King, not a president. His decrees are eternal laws, not legislation that representatives get to shape and adjust by compromise.

In a democracy, the target is personal liberty above all things. We want the government to get its hands off of us and let us follow our own consciences. Sometimes our attitude toward God, His Word, and His way of doing things is very similar. We want God to let us do what we want to do, and we buck whenever His Word contradicts our own desires or designs. We resound with the words of the Sons of Liberty, "Don't tread on me," instead of responding as the sons and daughters of God, who should be led by God's Spirit (Romans 8:14).

This applies to spiritual authority as well. The way God has structured the church and distributed leadership and influence throughout His kingdom does not follow a democratic pattern, but instead it follows the structure of a royal family. God has placed special anointing upon men and women in the body of Christ, not to elevate them to a position of superiority, but to humbly guard and protect the people of God, leading them into maturity. These positions are not there to dominate us or limit our freedoms. They are there to serve as coaches and guardrails of grace. If we see them as a threat instead of a gift, it may be that we are viewing a kingdom dynamic through our democratic bias.

When we say that we don't need leaders in our lives or that we refuse to submit our lives under spiritual authority, we become like white blood cells that turn on the body and begin to destroy our own immune system.

Submission may be viewed as a negative term or even an outdated concept according to some today, but it is very much a biblical word and kingdom concept. While every person, regardless of their maturity level, gender, giftedness, or economic status is equally loved and valued in the kingdom of God, not everyone has equal or equivalent roles in God's house. Submission does not mean less; submission indicates order.

Even King Jesus, the second person of the Trinity, fully and eternally God, submitted His life to the Father and to earthly parents and authorities as well. This is an astounding truth. He didn't submit because He was lesser than others. On the contrary, He was equal with God the Father as God and superior to every human being, but He willingly submitted Himself in order to bring God's salvation to you and me. He submitted to Mary and Joseph, because it was pleasing in God's sight. When it comes to you and me, we are called to live with the same attitude Christ had.

Let this mind be in you which was also in Christ Jesus, who being in the form of God, did not consider it robbery to be equal with God, but made himself of no reputation, taking the form of a bondservant, and coming in the likeness of men. And being found in appearance as a man, He humbled Himself and became obedient to the point of death, even the death of the cross."

—PHILIPPIANS 2:5–8, NKJV

God has established leaders in the body of Christ for our good. Just as Jesus submitted to leaders over Him while on Earth, we are called to honor those who are called to be spiritual overseers of our lives and faith. Though there has, at times, been abuse of authority by those who wield it, it does not excuse us from living *under cover.*

Submission is different than subjugation. Submission is not something that can be demanded by anyone. It is an inner attitude of the heart that must be offered to someone. It is not blindly following an individual or worshiping them as infallible, but it is honoring the calling and anointing upon those who are positioned in the kingdom for our benefit.

Just as we desire to have our gifts and callings recognized, it begins by honoring those who are ordained by God. We are only able to receive the spiritual transference of authority in the kingdom by honoring the authority God has entrusted to others. There is a reward awaiting us for how we respond to those in spiritual authority in God's house.

"He who receives you receives Me, and he who receives Me receives Him who sent Me. He who receives a prophet in the name of a prophet shall receive a prophet's reward. And he who receives a righteous man in the name of a righteous man shall receive a righteous man's reward."

—MATTHEW 10:40–42, NKJV

God has given fivefold ministry leaders of apostles, prophets, evangelists, pastors, and teachers in the body of Christ to mature us and bring us into our destiny in God. He has appointed elders and pastors in the church, not to rule as tyrants, but to serve as overseers and caretakers of our lives.

Remember those who rule over you, who have spoken the word of God to you, whose faith follow, considering the outcome of their conduct.

—Hebrews 13:7, nkjv

Shepherd the flock of God which is among you, serving as overseers, not by compulsion but willingly, not for dishonest gain but eagerly; nor as being lords over those entrusted to you, but being examples to the flock; and when the Chief Shepherd appears, you will receive the crown of glory that does not fade away.
Likewise you younger people, submit yourselves to your elders. Yes, all of you be submissive to one another, and be clothed with humility, for "God resists the proud, but gives grace to the humble."

—1 Peter 5:2–5, nkjv

In a self-styled world, we are called to demonstrate the order of the kingdom of God by honoring the leaders that God has ordained in the church and our lives. Recognizing and honoring all of the different spheres of authority that God has ordained is important for each member in the body of Christ to come into a mature mind-set and fulfill their unique and holy calling. When we resist His order and persist in our isolation, we stunt our own growth and potential.

Five Smooth Stones

When David went out to face the giant Philistine, Goliath, he didn't go with conventional armor or tactics. King Saul had offered David his own kingly armor but David rejected it in favor of the tools and techniques he learned as a shepherd. After all, David had spent years alone with God out in the wilderness, taking care of his father's sheep. During that process, God had developed David as a leader after His own heart. As this young leader walked down into the valley to face this intimidating enemy of Israel, he carried only a sling and a vision of who he was in God. He stooped down and, in what must've seemed a ridiculous move, pulled five smooth stones from the creek as the weapons of choice.

Then Saul clothed David with his armor. He put a helmet of bronze on his head and clothed him with a coat of mail, and David strapped his sword over his armor. And he tried in vain to go, for he had not tested them. Then David said to Saul, "I cannot go with these, for I have not tested them." So David put them off. Then he took his staff in his hand and chose five smooth stones from the brook and put them in his shepherd's pouch. His sling was in his hand, and he approached the Philistine.

—1 SAMUEL 17:38–40

The giant didn't understand what was about to happen to him because he was seeing through the corrupted lens of human power. Saul and the armies of Israel were about to witness the power of a man fully submitted to God and His ways. As David swung the stone in the sling, took aim, and let the stone fly, so too was David's destiny about to be unleashed. The rest, as they say, is biblical history!

Not only did God give young David a faith-filled strategy and five smooth stones with which to defeat the giant that stood between him and his destiny, but He's also given these weapons to His church and every member of it. Paul wrote to the church at Ephesus about God's strategy to strengthen the church and equip every member to discover and flourish in their purpose and calling.

But grace was given to each one of us according to the measure of Christ's gift. Therefore it says, "When He ascended on high he led a host of captives, and he gave gifts to men."

And He Himself gave some to be apostles, some prophets, some evangelists, and some pastors and teachers, for the equipping of the saints for the work of ministry, for the edifying of the body of Christ, till we all come to the unity of the faith and of the knowledge of the Son of God, to a perfect man, to the measure of the stature of the fullness of Christ; that we should no longer be children, tossed to and fro and carried about with every wind of doctrine, by the trickery of men, in the cunning craftiness of deceitful plotting, but, speaking the truth in love, may grow up in all things into Him who is the head—Christ—from whom the whole body, joined and knit together by what every joint supplies, according to the effective working by which every part does its share, causes growth of the body for the edifying of itself in love.

—EPHESIANS 4:8, ESV, 11–16, NKJV

The gifts that Christ gave to the church are the fivefold ministry offices, which are intended for the honing and equipping of the other members of the church. Serving as coaches and master builders, their unique anointing and leadership are essential for helping every other member of the body become effective, unified, and mature. These gifts, resident in these leaders, are intentional and essential, not optional. When a body is deficient in a nutrient, it can leave the body weak, sluggish, and ultimately diseased unto premature death. When a body is strong and thriving, the signs point to a respect, honor, and expectation for the spiritual impartation and anointing upon each specific fivefold office to bring maturity and completeness to each member. Let's briefly look deeper at each office and how it is designed to help us flourish.

What Are Apostles?

And He Himself gave some to be apostles...

—EPHESIANS 4:11, NKJV

The word *apostle* is a word that means "one commissioned to go or one sent on a mission." The original twelve apostles Jesus selected were the foundational stones upon which the church was established. They were entrusted as the first generation of leaders to preach the gospel to the nations and establish the church as the community of believers in every sphere.

Several of the original twelve, along with Saul who became Paul, were used by God to write most of the New Testament. Their power and authority were directly given by Jesus and recognized as authoritative by the early church and beyond.

There were others throughout the New Testament era who were also recognized as apostles beyond the original twelve. As mentioned, Paul became perhaps the most influential of all apostolic leaders as he traveled— teaching, writing, and establishing local churches and leaders throughout the entire Roman Empire. Other persons of note who were also referred to as apostles include James, Jesus's half-brother (James 1:19), Barnabas (Acts 14:14), Apollos (1 Corinthians 4:6–9), Timothy and Silvanus (1 Thessalonians 1:1; 2:6), Epaphroditus (Philippians 2:25), Andronicus, and a woman Junia (Romans 16:7).

Of course, the original twelve apostles of the Lamb will never be replaced in their significance or unique authority, but there have been those who walk in apostolic influence and anointing. You can find them throughout all of church history, present in every major vein or move of God whether they were called apostles or not.

Apostles or apostolic ministers play a vital role in the health and life of a local church. Ephesians 2:20 says that the office of the apostle, as well as the prophet, is foundational for strong church communities. Because they very often are used to start new churches, or strengthen existing churches, their influence is irreplaceable.

One of the key roles apostles or apostolic ministers carry is the ability to help identify those with leadership anointing on their life. We see this in Paul's life. He identifies a young man named Timothy while traveling through Derbe and Lystra. Timothy's mother was Jewish and his father a Greek, with a good reputation. When Paul met Timothy, he must've identified a calling in him that others were not able to see clearly. This is how an apostle works. They are able to see with a set of lenses other leadership offices do not possess. They can see spiritual super structures that will assist a pastor in growing, and they can see the gold inside an emerging leader.

> According to the grace of God given to me, like a skilled master builder I laid a foundation, and someone else is building upon it.
> —1 CORINTHIANS 3:10

> For though you have countless guides in Christ, you do not have many fathers. For I became your father in Christ Jesus through the gospel.
> —1 CORINTHIANS 4:15

We need fathers for our families to be healthy, and the church needs those who serve as fathers as well. Paul became a spiritual father to Timothy and several others in church leadership, even whole congregations. This is one of the unique roles of an apostle. Churches that are rightly related to the office of apostle have strength, stability, and the voice of a loving father who gives life to them and their leadership.

I am grateful for the apostolic voices that have influenced me personally, and the church I have had the privilege to lead. Never demanding a formal title or hierarchal level of control, I have had significant men of God who identified the gift in me from a very young age. These men have been mentors to me personally and have provided oversight to our congregation as a whole. One of the reasons we have been able to weather storms that inevitably come to a marriage and ministry is because Jane and I welcome apostolic influence. Men like Jimmy Evans, Tom Lane, Rick Renner, and Loren Covarrubias have been fathers in the faith to me and Radiant.

Apostles also bring encouragement to local churches as they teach and preach. They are able to connect a local congregation to the broader body of Christ and move of God. They remind individual members of the Great Commission and the importance to the whole that we all play. They are able to bring confirmation to the direction a leader is going, bringing increase and faith (Acts 16:5).

There is also an ability for an apostle to impart spiritual gifts and blessings, even their own spiritual authority and gifting, through the laying on of hands. Consider what the apostle Paul wrote to the church at Rome, where he desired to go as soon as possible. One of the reasons he desired to go there was to strengthen, encourage, and impart to them a spiritual gift.

> For I long to see you, that I may impart to you some spiritual gift to strengthen you—that is, that we may be mutually encouraged by each other's faith, both yours and mine.
> —Romans 1:11–12

This level of relationship is not possible from a distance. You can learn information from a livestream, podcast, or book, but it can never replace the face-to-face, in-person contact with the anointing. This is something that an entire generation stands to lose unless we restore the understanding of the fivefold ministry to the teachings that take place in the house of God.

Lastly, they are able to bring correction. When there is division, leadership issues, or doctrinal arguments threatening the unity of a church, the fatherly correction of an apostle can help bring order where there is chaos. This does not come from an authoritarian position, but from a servant-leadership role, coming up alongside the local eldership. Too many churches and believers alike are missing this gift that Jesus Himself gave to us for our maturity and destiny.

Profitable Prophets

And He Himself gave some to be apostles, some prophets…
—Ephesians 4:11, nkjv

Besides the gift of an apostle, the most misunderstood fivefold ministry office is that of the prophet. The grace office of prophet in the New Testament looks much different than the Old Testament caricature. In the Old Testament, with the exceptions of prophets, priests, and kings (and a few other exceptions), the people of God were not indwelled by the Holy Spirit to lead and guide them into all truth. The role of the prophet was the voice of God to everyone.

Today, we live on the other side of Pentecost—the fulfillment of God's promises that a day would come when He would pour His Spirit out on all flesh and that we would all be able to hear the voice of God.

"And it shall come to pass afterward, that I will pour out my Spirit on all flesh; your sons and your daughters shall prophesy, your old men shall dream dreams, and your young men shall see visions. Even on the male and female servants in those days I will pour out my Spirit."
—Joel 2:28–29

This was declared by Peter on the Day of Pentecost, the birth of the church. With the gift of the Holy Spirit making us a nation of priests and kings, the role of the prophet has shifted as well. Prophets still are gifted supernaturally to hear and see the heart and voice of God for His bride the church, but it is now subject to the eldership of the local church.

With that said, the office of the prophet is a valuable one that Paul identifies as foundational along with the office of apostle (Ephesians 2:20). They not only have the grace gift of prophecy (1 Corinthians 12), but they are also mature leaders, often working alongside apostles and other ministry offices to give direction, correction, and affirmation to the body of Christ. While every Christian can be used by God in the gift of prophecy—bringing edification, encouragement, and comfort (1 Corinthians 14:3)—it does not make them a prophet or someone who stands in a foundational office.

At Radiant Church, we have benefitted greatly from the ministry of prophets over the years. It seems very often that God will send them during times of transition or just before He is about to move in a significant way. We host something called Prophetic Presbytery every other year in which we bring in tested and mature prophets to minister over our congregation and individual candidates our elders select. They will prophesy over them without having ever met them, sharing God's heart for them and unlocking aspects of their calling, dreams, and destiny. Sometimes, a person who's been waiting for the timing of the Lord to launch out into a calling or to move in a desired direction is activated by the ministry of a prophet.

> Now there were in the church at Antioch prophets and teachers, Barnabas, Simeon who was called Niger, Lucius of Cyrene, Manaen a lifelong friend of Herod the tetrarch, and Saul. While they were worshiping the Lord and fasting, the Holy Spirit said, "Set apart for me Barnabas and Saul for the work to which I have called them." Then after fasting and praying they laid their hands on them and sent them off.
> —Acts 13:1–3

Not only is it encouraging for them, but also it is encouraging for the whole church. Pastors and leaders are able to get a sense of where we are as a body, and in many cases, we receive confirmation on the direction we have been sensing from the Lord. This is an invaluable gift from God that is missing in much of our American church paradigm.

On a personal level, words that have been spoken over Jane and me, sometimes decades ago, continually fuel us to press toward the call God has for us. There are many promises that were given though prophetic ministry years ago that are just now coming to fruition. Very often, I will go back through printed transcripts of prophetic words we received through tested prophetic ministry, and it will stir up my faith and strengthen me in the fight. This weapon of words is a significant part of the arsenal for every believer.

> This charge I entrust to you, Timothy, my child, in accordance with the prophecies previously made about you, that by them you may wage the good warfare.
>
> —1 TIMOTHY 1:18

Office of the Evangelist

> And He Himself gave some to be apostles, some prophets, some evangelists…
>
> —EPHESIANS 4:11, NKJV

Like all the other fivefold ministry offices, we are called to receive from the gift they carry as their primary anointing. The gifts that are associated with the fivefold ministry office gifts I am discussing here are resident in a lesser way in each believer, because we have the Holy Spirit abiding in us. The Holy Spirit is the anointing of Jesus, who is the Apostle of our faith, the Prophet greater than Moses, the Evangelist who first declared the good news of the gospel, and the great Shepherd and Teacher.

Every Christian has been sent on the Great Commission even if they are not an apostle in the technical sense of the word. Every Christian can prophesy in order to build others up, even if we have not been set in the office of a prophet. And each of us is called to share the good news, the gospel, wherever we have the opportunity, even if we do not carry the title of evangelist. The role of the evangelist is uniquely significant to the health of the local church.

> How beautiful upon the mountains are the feet of him who brings good news, who publishes peace, who brings good news of happiness, who publishes salvation, who says to Zion, "Your God reigns."
>
> —ISAIAH 52:7

The evangelist is a fisher of men, called to preach the simplicity of the gospel in order to win those who are far from Christ. Very often, this preaching is accompanied by great power, signs, and wonders that confirm the message of the cross.

Perhaps the most famous evangelist of our generation was Billy Graham. By all accounts, he is believed to have preached to more people in his lifetime than anyone who has ever lived.

The office of an evangelist is a laser-focused call, which not only adds new disciples to the kingdom of God but also serves as an adrenaline jolt into a body of believers to reach the lost and powerless.

If we are going to win the largest harvest of souls in our generation that the world has ever witnessed, we are going to need thousands of evangelists to rise up. I believe with all my heart that we will see this. And with almost seven billion souls alive on Planet Earth, it's unthinkable that God would not spur us on to pray, preach, and compel the nations to believe. We will need all evangelistic hands on deck—those who give their lives fully by traveling to the nations as well as those who are positioned in marketplace seats of influence.

Why Do We Need Pastors?

And He Himself gave some to be apostles, some prophets, some evangelists, some pastors...
—Ephesians 4:11, nkjv

I can't tell you how many times, over the years of being a pastor, I have been asked the question, why do we need pastors? More often than that, it has been put into a statement of fact instead of a question: "I don't need a pastor. I have the Holy Spirit and the Bible."

Unfortunately, this is not a rare belief. There are a lot of Christians that have a Lone Ranger mentality when it comes to their own relationship with God. They don't see the need for belonging to a church, and they sure don't see the need for a pastor to lead them or give them any level of accountability. This may seem like a very independent, mature attitude on the surface, but unfortunately, it is completely unbiblical.

It's true that every believer has the Holy Spirit and the Bible, but that does not negate or replace the role of a pastor or shepherd in our process. Pastors are elders who have been designated senior leader over a congregation with the responsibility to feed, lead, and protect the flock of God.

Pay careful attention to yourselves and to all the flock in which the Holy Spirit has made you overseers, to care for the church of

God, which he obtained with his own blood. I know that after my departure fierce wolves will come in among you, not sparing the flock, and from among your own selves will arise men speaking twisted things, to draw away the disciples after them.

—Acts 20:28–30

Notice who it was that Paul said appointed them. It was the Holy Spirit. The same Holy Spirit who inspired every word of the Scriptures. He appointed them through the apostles and other church leaders to oversee and care for the church.

In 1 Timothy 3, Paul gave specific qualifications for ones who should serve as overseers. To say we don't need a pastor in our lives is to tell the Holy Spirit He made a mistake. A pastor is a gift from God, not a chaperone or guardian given to govern our every decision. He is a feeder and a leader. It is our own responsibility, of course, to study the Scriptures, pray, do the work of an evangelist, and pursue the gifts and callings God has given us. We have a personal relationship with the Lord, and a pastor is not the intermediary between us and God. They are trainers, mentors, and coaches. They are anointed by God and appointed by men in order to equip the saints for the work of the ministry. This is precisely why we need pastors to care for us and guide us in this process.

Most of the time, when we buck the idea of submitting our lives to a pastor, it's not out of holy virtue but carnal vanity. An independent spirit is one that doesn't want to be subject to any level of correction. This spirit is prevalent in our culture and generation. In fact, I would say it's celebrated. Our maverick mind-sets can only serve to leave us vulnerable to deception and pride—the very things the devil loves to use to derail destinies.

So I exhort the elders among you, as a fellow elder and a witness of the sufferings of Christ, as well as a partaker in the glory that is going to be revealed; shepherd the flock of God that is among you, exercising oversight, not under compulsion, but willingly, as God would have you; not for shameful gain, but eagerly; not domineering over those in your charge, but being examples to the flock. And the chief Shepherd appears, you will receive the unfading crown of glory.

Likewise, you who are younger, be subject to the elders. Clothe yourselves, all of you, with humility toward one another, for "God opposes the proud but gives grace to the humble."

—1 Peter 5:1–5

Not only does Peter give instruction to pastors about their methods and motives as leaders, he also encourages believers to recognize their authority and honor them from the heart. Obviously, there are some leaders who have taken advantage of the God-given influence for personal gain or got caught up in power trips, but this does not negate the significance of this office. We have seen this kind of abuse, not just in the church, but in every sphere of leadership. This is not only a pastor or church issue. This is a human sinfulness issue.

You need a pastor. You cannot flourish in your calling and destiny without having someone in your life to which you have submitted the process of your development. That's not to say that you won't go to heaven without going to church or having a pastor. That would be ridiculous and equally dangerous. We are completely saved by grace through faith.

But it does mean that the purposes that heaven has for you will be difficult to maneuver without a shepherd, leading the way through treacherous spiritual terrain, helping to graciously lead you out of the world and into that calling. There is no progress without process, and there is no process without a pastoral voice.

The Office of the Teacher

And He Himself gave some to be apostles, some prophets, some evangelists, and some pastors and teachers...

—Ephesians 4:11, nkjv

The final fivefold ministry gift to the church is that of the teacher. It is often combined with the office of pastor because a pastor must also be able to teach (1 Timothy 3:2). I believe that the role of the teacher, though, is a specific leadership gifting, unique unto itself. A teacher is gifted, not necessarily to govern like a pastor or an apostle, but they are gifted with the ability to dig deep into the Scriptures and teach the Word in a life-transforming way. They are the gourmet chefs of the kingdom, preparing exquisite feasts out of God's Word. They teach not only the foundational doctrines of Christ (Hebrews 6), but they also move beyond surface revelations and dive deep into the waters of the Spirit of truth like a Master Diver.

I am so thankful for the many voices of the teacher office that have fed me over the years. Men and women like Rick Renner and Beth Moore who have invested their lives into stoking a passion for the Word of God in the hearts of His people. I am also grateful for the lesser-known teachers who serve in the local church of whom no one outside of their congregation may ever hear. Nevertheless, they teach Sunday School classes and Bible studies and strengthen new believers in the water of the Word. These are unsung heroes, but they are in no way overlooked in heaven.

In our day and in our nation, there are ironically more Bibles than people. We have more translations available than ever before. We even have the Bible on our smartphones and tablets. Yet, biblical illiteracy is at an all-time high. The enemy loves to operate in this type of darkness and ignorance. This is why, now more than ever, we need the teacher office fully functioning in the local church.

> Now the Spirit expressly says that in the later times some will depart from the faith by devoting themselves to deceitful spirits and teachings of demons.
> —1 Timothy 4:1

Satan does his best work of corruption and deception where there is no revelation. The teacher is God's gift to the church, which is hungry for the Word of God. Teachers impart and provoke within us greater revelation and a stronger desire to study the Scriptures for ourselves. As we cry out to the Lord, "Show us Your ways," as Moses did (Exodus 33:13), He raises up teachers for the body of Christ. When we recognize and embrace our need for a teacher, we position ourselves to grow strong in His Word.

Like all great teachers and mentors, a true teacher who stands in the five-fold ministry office does not desire dependency upon themselves. Instead, the teacher hopes to develop a heart in all of their students to learn as they have. The same Holy Spirit Jesus promised would lead and guide us into all truth (John 16:13) is resident in each believer, ready to open our eyes to the treasures of God's Word if we will only open our hearts and Bibles.

God's Greenhouse

Now that we see in more detail that the fivefold ministry offices are actually gifts of God that help prepare us for our destiny, it's important that we also see how they fit together within the local church to create an environment of flourishing. The way I would describe the spiritual design of a church is like that of a greenhouse—a spiritual greenhouse.

As we have seen in Ephesians 4, God's desire is for each of us to grow up as mature believers, fully equipped to do the work of the ministry He has specifically designed us for. We also see that we grow best when we are developing together, under the leadership of those who are anointed by God to train and equip us. When this happens, the Bible describes this process as "The whole body joined and held together by every joint with which it is equipped, when each part is working properly, makes the body grow so that it builds itself up in love" (Ephesians 4:16).

A good friend of ours owns a greenhouse business. In the spring, they open their doors for the public to come in to buy beautiful plants and flowers to landscape their yards. Their place is packed with people who are finally coming out of their homes after a long Michigan winter, excited for the warmer weather and the coming summer, buying everything available.

What most people don't realize is that Darren and his family work for months to prepare for this moment. All winter long, they create and maintain an environment conducive for plants and flowers to grow. That means it must be warm inside when it's freezing outside. It must be humid inside when it's dry and harsh outside. The plants must be exposed to sunlight even when the winter months are dreary.

The greenhouse is an incubator of life. It enables the process of seeds to roots to shoots to take place in an environment that is intentionally created in the midst of the opposite natural environment in order to produce superior results. This is what the church is.

The local church is a kingdom greenhouse, establishing countercultural conditions in order to produce supernatural fruitfulness and maturity.

All around us, decay is taking its toll, but in the church, believers are being equipped, unified, filled with the Spirit, and built up in love. As disciples, we are becoming fruitful and prepared to do great exploits as we encounter the presence of the Lord.

It takes a lot of effort to create and manage a greenhouse. It takes a lot of grace to create a healthy church environment in which Christians grow and flourish.

Giving Ourselves to the Process

Each of us has a destiny and purpose we are created to fulfill. Each of us has been saved and called, and not with an ordinary calling but with what the Bible calls "a holy calling" (2 Timothy 1:9). Destiny is not something that just a few elite Christians get and the rest of us are left to just wait on the tarmac until we go to heaven. God has a destiny for each one of us.

There is, however, a difference between having a calling and a God-given destiny and actually fulfilling it. Jesus was clear when He said, "Many are called but few are chosen" (Matthew 22:14). Everyone receives a call, an invitation into God's preferred plan for our lives. We become chosen, or qualified, when we say yes to the process. There is no destiny without the process. The whole purpose of the different ministry gifts within the environment of the church is to host the process by which the Holy Spirit shapes, prepares, and takes us from glory to glory.

Submitting our lives to others is really submitting our lives to God's process. The example of Jesus is that His exaltation came on the other side of His willingness to humble Himself and go through the pain and agony of the cross in order to fulfill God's purpose.

> Have this mind among yourselves, which is yours in Christ Jesus, who, though he was in the form of God, did not count equality with God a thing to be grasped, but emptied himself, by taking the form of a servant, being born in the likeness of men. And being found in human form, he humbled himself by becoming obedient to the point of death, even death on a cross. Therefore God has highly exalted him and bestowed on him the name that is above every name, so that at the name of Jesus every knee should bow, in heaven and on earth and under the earth, and every tongue confess that Jesus Christ is Lord, to the glory of God the Father.
> —PHILIPPIANS 2:5–11

Humility is the fertilizer for destiny. It accelerates the process in every way. Fertilizer is made from living things that die and so is humility. When we willingly die to ourselves and become low, entrusting our future and our calling to the Lord, we actually position ourselves for promotion in a stronger way than if we are motivated by ambition, pride, or fear. These elements are acidic to the spirit and will kill whatever good is growing in us. Humility feeds the seeds of greatness inside our spiritual DNA.

> Clothe yourselves, all of you, with humility toward one another, for "God opposes the proud but gives grace to the humble." Humble yourselves, therefore, under the mighty hand of God so that at the proper time he may exalt you, casting all your anxieties on him, because he cares for you.
>
> —1 Peter 5:5–7

Notice Peter says humility is something only we can choose for ourselves. No one can make us choose humility. The opposite of choosing humility is experiencing humiliation. Humility happens when we willingly lower ourselves. Humiliation is the painful result when we rise up in pride and entitlement, only to be brought low by circumstances.

This attitude of humility is the essential nutrient that activates our destiny and allows our taproots to go deep into the soil of the kingdom. Without it, we stay shallow, looking for the instant promotion, recognition, or someone to see how great we are. There is no shortcut to destiny. You will never find it on the sale rack. Destiny is never discounted; you have to pay full price for it and that requires process.

Chapter Nine
FLOURISH IN YOUR PROCESS

When I was a young man armed with the knowledge that I was called to serve the Lord in full-time ministry, I had very little understanding about the process. I thought that, if God had called me and gifted me, I should immediately have open doors of opportunity to exercise my gift and be hired by a church. I was called, talented, and as you can tell, humble (tongue firmly in cheek). I thought that, if there was perhaps a process, it included going to Bible college for most, but I had spent hundreds of hours as a teenager studying the Bible. I was attending a small Bible college in my hometown, but to be honest, it seemed to be taking a long time to get through, and I wanted to get going with my destiny.

The Lord was so gracious to me during this period of my life, teaching me patiently the way of the kingdom, so that I could eventually flourish in His courts. He taught me so many things about who He was, who I was, and how my character needed to be refined through some painful moments of process that today I am thankful for.

I was attending a wonderful church that was really beginning to experience some real growth. I was serving in the youth ministry while attending Bible college on the other side of town. I would drive over many afternoons to volunteer alongside the youth pastor who kindly had agreed to mentor me. After several weeks of doing this, he invited me to do an internship at the church. This was it! The moment my gifting was finally being recognized and received.

I showed up on the first day with my little white Isuzu Impulse full of my theology books, wearing a crisp white shirt and tie (that's what pastors wore, right?) ready to do "ministry."

When I walked into the offices, I found the senior pastor and asked him in which office I should put all of my books and what time would we all get together to study and talk theology.

He gave me the strangest look and told me that I wouldn't need my books. He asked me if I had any other clothes that I could work in.

Confused, I said, "Well, I've got some basketball shorts and tennis shoes out in the car but..."

He told me to go get changed and meet him downstairs by the shed.

Once I had changed and found him, he handed me a broom and directed my attention to the massive parking lot that was covered with brick dust from the recent building project. He told me that my first job was to sweep the parking lot completely clean and then come find him. He went back to his office, and I was left confused, thinking, "This isn't ministry! This is a waste of my time. Doesn't he know that I am called to do the work of the ministry?"

Nevertheless, I started to sweep the parking lot and began to think about all the reasons that this was a disappointment when, suddenly, it hit me! I understood what he was trying to teach me. I dropped the broom and went up to his office with bated breath.

"I get it!" I said. "I know what you're trying to teach me!"

He looked quite annoyed when he asked me what I was talking about.

"It's a parable, right?" I said. "The kingdom of heaven is like a dirty parking lot, and the gospel is like the broom. We must preach the gospel boldly until all the earth is swept clean of sin!" (This really happened!)

Somehow I was picturing this as a Karate Kid moment, where I was being taught to wax on and wax off in order to get to the real stuff of ministry.

The pastor kindly looked at me and said, "No, that's not what it means. When I asked you to sweep the parking lot, it was because the parking lot needs sweeping, and you can't become a leader in the church until you are willing to serve in any capacity that is needed."

This is an embarrassing story now, but it was an important lesson then. God was teaching me humility and servanthood through the process of making progress. I am grateful for that lesson and all the others I learned along the way because they enabled me to overcome my immaturity and false perspectives about ministry.

God uses parking lots and pits to draw our destinies to the surface.

Timing Is Everything

Allow me to draw your attention back to an important foundational scripture in 1 Peter 5:5–7. It states that when we "humble ourselves under the mighty hand of God," we position ourselves for God to promote us "at the proper time."

You see, in the kingdom, timing is everything. God speaks to us and plants the seeds of gifting and destiny from the vantage point of eternity. But those seeds must go through a process within time in order to come to maturity. This process is called seedtime and harvest.

Peter, the apostle who wrote this portion of the New Testament, understood personally what that process was like. A very boisterous, self-confident leader, he had spent three years walking in person with Jesus as one of His three closest disciples. Peter was far more confident in his own readiness to reign and rule as an apostle than his process indicated he was. On the night Jesus was arrested, Peter told Jesus he would never deny Him and was ready to fight to the finish and was even ready to die with Jesus. But the Lord knew exactly where Peter was in the process of preparation.

> Then Jesus said to them, "You will all fall away because of me this night. For it is written, 'I will strike the shepherd, and the sheep of the flock will be scattered.' But after I am raised up, I will go before you to Galilee."
> Peter answered him, "Though they all fall away because of you, I will never fall away."
> Jesus said to him, "Truly, I tell you, this very night, before the rooster crows, you will deny me three times."
> Peter said to him, "Even if I must die with you, I will not deny you!"
> And all the disciples said the same.
> —Matthew 26:31–35

In the following days, Peter would be confronted with how much pride he had and how un-ready he really was. It wouldn't be until after the resurrection that, with a humble heart finally, Peter would be restored and commissioned by Jesus to "feed My sheep." Peter's process would require him to spend forty more days with Jesus, seeing Him in light of His resurrection power in order to truly understand the kingdom of God and his purpose in it.

Peter had operated in the supernatural throughout his training days, but when the Day of Pentecost had fully come, the Holy Spirit would fill this vessel, who had gone through the process of refining. And on this day, Peter would deliver the most powerful sermon and altar call the world had ever known. From a fisherman in Galilee to an apostle in Jerusalem, Peter became a pillar of the church.

Paul is another example of process. We all know about his pedigree before becoming a Christian. Paul was a brilliant Jewish leader, being groomed to sit on the Sanhedrin council that ruled the nation of Israel. He was trained under the leading scholar of his day, Gamaliel. Paul was zealous for the faith and militant in his dedication against all its enemies, including the church.

> ... though I myself have reason for confidence in the flesh also. If anyone else thinks he has reason for confidence in the flesh, I have more: circumcised on the eighth day, of the people of Israel, of the tribe of Benjamin, a Hebrew of Hebrews; as to the law, a Pharisee; as to zeal, a persecutor of the church; as to righteousness under the law, blameless.
> —PHILIPPIANS 3:4–6

But after an encounter with the risen Lord on the road to Damascus, Saul of Tarsus's life would never be the same. His name was changed to Paul, and he was radically humbled and called with one of the most dramatic callings in biblical history. The Lord set him apart unto apostolic ministry to the nations of the world. With all of his training and experience, you would think Paul would instantly step into a leadership role as an apostle of note. But, instead, Paul became an apostle of *not*. Not yet, that is. You see, it would take many years, more than fourteen, between Paul's calling and Paul's commissioning at Antioch.

> Now there were in the church at Antioch prophets and teachers, Barnabas, Simeon who was called Niger, Lucius of Cyrene, Manaen a lifelong friend of Herod the tetrarch, and Saul. While they were worshiping the Lord and fasting, the Holy Spirit said, "Set apart for me Barnabas and Saul for the work to which I

have called them." Then after fasting and praying they laid their hands on them and sent them off.

—ACTS 13:1–3

What was Paul doing between his calling and being activated and released into it? He was serving in a local church, submitting to its leadership, and going through the process of development and maturity. Once he was launched, the fruit of his ministry became unparalleled. The reason he was so fruitful and his ministry flourished in the midst of some of the most difficult surroundings and persecutions is because Paul had submitted to the process.

The Bible is replete with the stories of men and women like Joseph, Moses, Joshua, Daniel, Esther, Deborah, David, and many others who *became* heroes of the faith. They were not made of a more superior stock than any normal person, but they went through a superior process of development through which they chose humility.

Hell's Greatest Weapon

There is a weapon the devil wields masterfully in order to keep God's children from submitting to His process of maturity and flourishing in their calling. It is the toxin of bitterness that is caused by offense. Nothing can delay or ultimately destroy a destiny quicker than this poison of the soul. Proverbs 18:19 says, "An offended friend is harder to win back than a fortified city" (NLT).

In my experience as a pastor, offense is a nuclear weapon against the unity, destiny, and potential of the body of Christ. It causes division between believers and isolates members of the same body, keeping them from coming together in catalytic momentum. We will never truly become mature representations of Christ on Earth, walking in the fullness of the stature of Christ, if we are tainted by offense and poisoned by bitterness.

The writer of Hebrews talks explicitly about the dangers of becoming offended and the ramifications it can have on our kingdom calling and destiny.

> Now no chastening seems to be joyful for the present, but painful; nevertheless, afterward it yields the peaceable fruit of righteousness to those who have been trained by it.

Therefore strengthen the hands which hang down, and the feeble knees, and make straight paths for your feet, so that what is lame may not be dislocated, but rather be healed. Pursue peace with all people, and holiness, without which no one will see the Lord: looking carefully lest anyone fall short of the grace of God; lest any root of bitterness springing up cause trouble, and by this many become defiled; lest there be any fornicator or profane person like Esau, who for one morsel of food sold his birthright. For you know that afterward, when he wanted to inherit the blessing, he was rejected, for he found no place for repentance, though he sought it diligently with tears.

—HEBREWS 12:11–17, NKJV

Here, the Jewish believers were being encouraged not to let up in their race to follow Jesus. The process of discipline they were experiencing was the result of God's love not of His cruelty or absence. God is a Father and, like all fathers, wants to see His children grow up and be strong, confident, and effective sons and daughters, walking in their callings. Children don't always understand why they have to go through these lessons. They just want to speed up the process and get to the good stuff.

We all have dreams in our hearts. That is the way God has designed us. Our imaginations are the canvas upon which the vision of our lives, futures, and destinies is painted upon. But on the same canvas God shows us His prophetic vision for our lives, the devil paints from a pallet of alternative colors. God's color scheme is grace, hope, love, and faith. The devil paints with pride, discouragement, fear, jealousy, and doubt. When it seems that it's taking too long for the paint of God's destiny to dry, we become susceptible to losing heart and becoming offended.

Satan uses the imagery of members of a body who are weak or unstable and can easily get pulled out of joint. Sprains happen when joints that connect different body parts are twisted or forced to move in a direction that is not natural to them or goes against the direction they were moving. This causes dislocation. If you've ever dislocated a finger or sprained an ankle, you know how unplanned and how painful those moments are. The connecting tissue is stretched beyond its natural limits, and immediately, pain shoots throughout your entire body.

This imagery is a perfect portrayal of how offense works in the body. Two members working together, held together at the joint, experience a conflict that stretches their relational tendons beyond what is normal. The immediate pain causes them to isolate and shut down. With the example of a physical sprain, if we do not immediately get it looked at by a doctor, it can become inflamed, infected and not heal correctly. If believers aren't quick to get their relationships restored when wrongs have been committed or offenses occur, individual members will be in danger of bitterness setting in.

Offenses between members of the church family are not the only relationships that can be damaged. It's possible for us to become offended at God Himself. When God doesn't take us on the path we planned, doesn't answer our prayers the way we wanted, or does take longer than we thought our process should take, we can become offended. The religious leaders of Jesus's day were the prime example of becoming offended toward God's purposes and methods.

> Then the disciples came and said to him, "Do you know that the Pharisees were offended when they heard this saying?" He answered, "Every plant that my heavenly Father has not planted will be rooted up. Let them alone; they are blind guides. And if the blind lead the blind, both will fall into a pit."
> —MATTHEW 15:12–14

Jesus didn't do things the way the religious leaders thought the Messiah would do them. He didn't affirm their methodology or timeline, and so they became offended. Jesus said that their offense had literally caused them to become blind spiritually—and that everyone who followed them would end up in the pit as well. The pit is always a picture in the Bible of being imprisoned or constrained. They were now unable to fulfill their purpose and calling as spiritual leaders because of their offense at God.

Selling Out Our Birthright

Esau is the example that the writer of Hebrews uses to depict how offense works to derail our destiny. We discussed Jacob and Esau at the beginning of this book. Let's take another look at their story but through a different lens.

Esau was a man with a godly heritage and a covenant promise. As the firstborn of his father Isaac, he was set to inherit all of Isaac's wealth and also the spiritual blessing of the Abrahamic covenant. He had everything anyone in his position could've wanted, but instead he became offended and bitter at the process.

One day when he had come in from a long hunt, Esau was hungry. Jacob had made a pot of lentil stew, and Esau wanted some. Jacob took advantage of his brother by bartering a bowl of bean soup for his birthright. (See Genesis 25:29–34.)

Notice that it was when Esau was weary after his hunt that he was willing to give up his inheritance for immediate gratification. When we are living in pursuit of our own destinies and become weary in the process, the deceiver comes and offers us a shortcut. It's in this place of exhaustion, discouragement, fear, or isolation that we are tempted to despise or trade out our destiny for what is easy and convenient. But whether or not we are able to stand against the enemy is all connected to our process of development and maturity.

God uses the process of refinement to prepare us for our ultimate purpose. Our purpose or destiny is not a single level or event—it is who we become on the other side of the process. God is much more concerned with who we become inwardly than He is in what we do outwardly.

Esau became bitter and never recovered. He married outside the covenant and became isolated from his brother and family. He became defiled.

How many Christians lose their birthright and the opportunity to flourish in the courts of God and bear fruit even in their old age because their soul gets sprained and their dream becomes dislocated through offense? How ineffective does the body of Christ as a whole become when there are members missing and not adding their contribution to the family of God in the household of faith? I think the issue is not exceptional; I believe it is epidemic!

I can't tell you of the countless people who have become shipwrecked and begun to live immorally after an offense yet had, at one time, been serving the Lord zealously. Many believers have left the church hurt, upset, and offended and never return to fellowship. This is why Hebrews encourages us to strive for peace with everyone *and* for holiness. Offenses will come, guaranteed. Jesus said it was inevitable.

Then said he unto the disciples, It is impossible but that offences will come: but woe unto him, through whom they come!

—LUKE 17:1, KJV

Understanding the Trap of Offense

It's important that we understand the nature and modus operandi of offense in order to avoid it. The word *offense* is the Greek word *skandalon*. It is where we get the word *scandal* from. Its technical meaning is the trigger point of a trap. Once the prey pulls or takes the bait from the trap, the cage collapses on the catch mechanism, and the prey is caught or killed.

This is how offense works. The enemy deceives us when we are vulnerable because we are angry, weary, or discouraged. He offers us a shortcut, like a bowl of lentil soup, and convinces us that this is the appropriate option. When we take the bait and become offended, we also become trapped. Paul calls it falling "short of the grace of God" (Romans 3:23). This doesn't necessarily mean that we "lose" our salvation, but it does mean we can lose our birthright or inheritance. The grace of God is what empowers us toward our destiny. It is what lubricates our soul to be able to endure difficulties and overcome friction in relationships when things heat up. God gives us grace when we humble ourselves, but when we take the bait of the devil, we fall short of that.

Grace is a seed that takes root in our hearts, enabling us to bear fruit and flourish. Offense is a weed that puts a tap root down into our soul, poisoning us with bitterness. The fruit that it bears is beautiful but toxic. Everyone around us becomes contaminated because they unknowingly are eating the fruit of our lives—either unto life and destiny or unto offense and sin.

There are three progressive levels of offense that steal a believer's birthright and keep them from flourishing in God.

Level #1: Isolation

The first level is isolation. When an offense takes place, our first reaction is to shut down relationally. We want to put space between us and the one who injured us or the one who we perceive is not cooperating with our desired outcome. The Book of Proverbs speaks wisely about the intent and outcome of isolating ourselves.

> A man who isolates himself seeks his own desire; he rages against all wise counsel.
>
> —Proverbs 18:1, NKJV

Notice what the motive is? We isolate because we want what we want. We turn from pursuing God's will to our will. When our will is aligned with God's will, the impossible becomes probable. When we isolate, even from God, our will becomes weaponized and can threaten our destiny. At this level, we aren't looking for wisdom or even godly answers. We just want to stay to ourselves because we know if we draw near to the Lord or allow ourselves to be vulnerable, He will send wise voices to speak into our lives and we may not like what they have to say to us. Isolation leads to the second level of offense.

Level #2: Dislocation

Dislocation occurs when one part of the body is not able to cooperate with the rest of the body. It needs to be put back into place and held tightly in order to let the body heal it. It may require some time and tenderness. When Paul said, "If one member suffers, all suffer together" (1 Corinthians 12:26), I think we can all relate.

When you have an injury, even a small one, it affects the rest of your activities and function. An injury to your small toe can affect your walk. One dislocated joint can affect the entire body and requires attention and healing. If a part of the body is left unhealed or a bone unset, it can cause infection or even atrophy. If this happens, it can eventually lead to disease or death.

In a spiritual sense, similar circumstances happen far too often in the body of Christ. We cut ourselves off. We stop serving, stop going to church, and stop giving. Whenever these things happen, it's a telltale sign that offense has taken root and can potentially lead to the third and final level of offense.

Level #3: Captivation

This is the ultimate desire of the devil. He wants to get you so offended that you isolate yourself and cut yourself off from the vine of fellowship. He knows that the soil of the house of God is perfect for growing sons and daughters who are flourishing and thus a threat to the blueprint of hell for their lives. Offense is the perfect trap.

Wolves love to hunt sheep. They will stalk them and identify the weak and isolated among the flock and encircle them at the right moment. Once they are cut off from the rest of the sheep, there isn't much that can be done to save them. This is how the devil works to steal, kill, and destroy.

> God may perhaps grant them repentance leading to a knowledge of the truth, and they may come to their senses and escape from the snare of the devil, after being captured by him to do his will.
> —2 TIMOTHY 2:25–26

The bait of offense is always connected to our desires and our wills. The devil always offers freedom from constraints, discipline, and pain under the guise of "do it your way" or "you deserve" this or that. His payoff, however, is never liberty but captivity.

The word *repentance* seems harsh to many who have been wounded or offended either by others or God Himself. Some may have said, "How could God be so cruel to tell me to repent. Doesn't He know how badly it hurts?"

To repent means to have a change of heart or make a change in the path you are going down. Esau sought repentance years later after becoming offended, but the damage had been done. He was sorrowful, but his heart was so hard that he could not find his way back to his birthright. I am grateful for the grace of God that goes further than we would ever imagine, chasing us down even. Still, we should be sober about how dangerous offense is to our destinies.

The Antidote for Offense

For every toxin there is an antitoxin. If you've ever watched those emergency room television shows and seen what happens when someone gets bitten by a snake, then you understand how time is of the essence. If it

144

was a leg that was bitten, it quickly becomes inflamed and swollen. The situation can go bad fast until the leg needs to be amputated. Once the antivenom is injected, the toxic effects begin to reverse, and the immune system is able to fight the disease and bring the leg back to health.

It is almost inevitable that we will at some point become offended on our way toward maturity and destiny. It's not an issue of avoiding it; it's more important that we know the antidote when it happens. When God disappoints us, delays us, and sometimes allows us to be injured by another believer, how do we respond? The antidote to offense is humility and teachability.

We've discussed humility and pride, how God says that He actually resists the proud. But what about the role of teachability? I have found that if you are humble and teachable, you also become unoffendable. Humility is seeing through the lens of gratitude and grace. Remembering who we were when God's grace first met us and then reminding our hearts how great our God is will dramatically impact how we respond to things we feel we are entitled to or how we feel when others mistreat us. We will realize that we are all works in progress. It is Jesus who is the Author and the Finisher of our faith. Most of us are somewhere in the middle of our story, and Jesus isn't done writing.

Teachability is one of the most overlooked and underestimated virtues in the body of Christ. We celebrate talent, laud performance, and exalt confidence but forget about the potency of teachability. Connected to teachability is a submissive attitude. Submission is another way of saying that we are coming under the authority or influence of another. We view submission as weakness, but it is actually strength demonstrated through wisdom.

So much of our offense comes out of unmet expectations or disappointment based upon what we think we deserve or how things should go for us in the process. This becomes a breeding ground for the bacteria of bitterness to grow in the dark places of our souls. We compare where we are in our journey of faith against what other people are getting and become discouraged and envious.

Who is wise and understanding among you? Let him show by good conduct that his works are done in the meekness of wisdom. But if you have bitter envy and self-seeking in your hearts, do not boast and lie against the truth. This wisdom does not descend from above, but is earthly, sensual, demonic. For where envy and self-seeking exist, confusion and every evil thing are there.

—James 3:13–16, nkjv

But the opposite is also true. When we bring our disappointment to the Lord instead of hiding it and when we willingly submit our lives and our process to God and do not let the devil come and plant his seed of offense in our soul, the enemy is pushed back, and we can be cleansed and purified. This is the process of flourishing. Submitting to God is an aggressive posture of war against the enemy of your destiny. We fight from our knees in humility and teachability.

But he gives more grace. Therefore it says, "God opposes the proud, but gives grace to the humble." Submit yourselves therefore to God. Resist the devil, and he will flee from you. Draw near to God, and He will draw near to you. Cleanse your hands, you sinners, and purify your hearts, you double-minded.

—James 4:6–8

Confidence in the Process

The reason we can flourish in the process of development in our lives is because we know the faithfulness of God is a constant. Men may let us down, and we may even let ourselves down with bad decisions and failures, but God will never let us down. His purposes will not be thwarted in your life, as long as you stay submitted to God and walk in the steps that He has ordained for you. He has promised that what He has started in you He will also finish.

And I am sure of this, that he who began a good work in you will bring it to completion at the day of Jesus Christ."

—Philippians 1:6

Staying teachable in the process and staying planted in the environment of the church are the keys to promotion and walking in your birthright. God may not be the cause of every challenge or point of conflict you experience in the journey, but rest assured, He is using everything for your good and your calling.

There is pain in the process, but this is the way of the kingdom. We are not called to be like those who live attempting to avoid pain. We are called to fulfill our destinies. We are not called to arrive safely at death, but we are called to leave it all out on the field. We can trust that when our roots are deep in the house of the Lord, not allowing our hearts to become offended and uprooted, that God is at work behind the scenes and between the lines, perfecting us in the process.

I love the words Joseph, a man acquainted with the pain and process, said to his brothers, years after they sold him into slavery. Refusing to become bitter, he allowed God to finish the process. Then he trusted that the God of his dream would bring it to fulfillment. When he stood in the position of power and his dream had become his destiny, he said to those who had harmed him:

> But Joseph said to them, "Do not fear, for am I in the place of God? As for you, you meant evil against me, but God meant it for good, to bring it about that many people should be kept alive, as they are today. So do not fear, I will provide for you and your little ones." Thus he comforted them and spoke kindly to them.
>
> —GENESIS 50:19–21

Chapter Ten
FLOURISH IN YOUR LEGACY

A few years ago, I made a trip up to the city I was raised in and to the church I grew up in as a teenager. First Assembly in Grand Rapids, Michigan, was my spiritual home throughout my formative teen years. I had encountered the Lord there many times, sat through hundreds of hours of teaching, filled numerous journals, and responded to multiple altar calls.

I wanted to return to this altar to recount all that God had done in my life in those formative years, before I was a pastor or anything other than a "son," and listen to what the Lord would say to me now on this holy ground. I went into the balcony and found the pew I was sitting in during one memorable service when I responded to an altar call, dedicating my life to serve God in full-time ministry.

As I sat in the silence, reflecting back to that moment and being incredibly grateful for this church's impact upon my life, I heard the whisper of the Holy Spirit say to me, "You are here today because of those who came before you."

I was stunned. I asked the Lord who He was speaking of, and He said to me, "You don't know them, but I know each of them. You and the others impacted in this place over the years are part of their legacy."

In that moment, I realized I was not the only one who had been impacted by the Lord in this room. There were countless people and numerous generations that had made it possible for that church to be there when a young teenage boy showed up looking for a spiritual home. I sat there and thought of the different families I remembered and imagined the names and faces of those who I had never met who prayed, gave, and labored to build such an environment. What a legacy they left.

It made me grateful and also aware that each of us determines what kind of legacy we leave to the generations that come after us. Often, when we think about legacy, we think specifically about our kids and grandchildren. But what if there is a generational legacy that we leave in the house of God? Psalm 92, the foundational scripture for this book, speaks about this legacy:

The righteous flourish like the palm tree and grow like a cedar in Lebanon. They are planted in the house of the Lord: they flourish in the courts of our God. They still bear fruit in old age; they are ever full of sap and green, to declare that the Lord is upright; He is my rock, and there is no unrighteousness in him.

—PSALM 92:12–15

Part of what it means to flourish in the house of God, is to build a generational legacy beyond ourselves and continue to flourish in our older years because we put deep roots down in our younger years. We live in a culture that celebrates youthfulness and believes that almost anything beyond the age of fifty is preparation to retire. This is not the way of the kingdom. God wants the church to be a multi-generational house that passes down a legacy from one generation to another.

Compounded Blessing

God revealed Himself in the Old Testament as the God of Abraham, Isaac, and Jacob. The full expression of God's covenant promises to Abraham required three generations to see them come to completeness. In the same way, I believe God has designed the church in such a way that the fullness of the house of God is revealed when there are three generations all flourishing in the same house together. This is important because each generation has something to bring to the table that the other generation draws life from.

There is a complete picture of what it looks like when each of the generations offer honor to the other. John, the aged and last-surviving apostle, wrote to the church in his first epistle about the importance of a multigenerational legacy:

> I am writing to you, little children, because your sins are forgiven for his name's sake.
> I am writing to you, fathers, because you know him who is from the beginning.
> I am writing to you, young men, because you have overcome the evil one.
> I write to you, children, because you know the Father.

I write to you, fathers, because you know him who is from the
beginning.
I write to you, young men, because you are strong, and the word
of God abides in you, and you have overcome the evil one.
—1 JOHN 2:12–14

He identifies the three generations: fathers, young men, and children.
Three levels of maturity. The youngest are strong and zealous. The middle
generation has victorious testimonies that build the faith of the spiritual
children, and the fathers have the years of intimate knowledge from walking
with the Lord through the maturation process. When the strengths of each
generation meet each other, there is a compounded blessing. The psalmist
called this the commanded blessing.

Behold, how good and pleasant it is when brothers dwell in
unity! It is like the precious oil on the head, running down
on the beard, on the beard of Aaron, running down on the
collar of his robes! It is like the dew of Hermon, which falls on
the mountains of Zion! For there the Lord has commanded the
blessing. Life forevermore.
—PSALM 133

When there is a divine flow of testimony and anointing from one generation to the next, in unity, this is what you call a legacy. At the heart of it,
the church is a family. When there is order in the family, blessing is passed
down. Each generation owns the responsibility to fulfill their purpose but
also to leave an inheritance to the next generation. We don't just view the
church as a utilitarian institution but a household worth investing in.

One generation shall praise Your works to another, and shall
declare Your mighty acts.
—PSALM 145:4, NKJV

What Does a Flourishing Legacy Look Like?

Everybody thinks about what their legacy will be one day. What will
people say about you at your funeral? What will be written on the grave-
stone after you have stepped into eternity? In our youthfulness, we may not
give a lot of thought to our legacies, but as we get older and we realize how

short our earthly life is, we begin to take stock of who we are and what we have done. There is no greater legacy that can be left than a legacy of faithfulness to the Lord, exemplified by a life planted and flourishing in the house of the Lord.

Of all the things we could leave our children and children's children, leaving them a healthy church that is the soil where kingdom potential can thrive and come to life, is perhaps the greatest.

Stocks, bonds, properties, and material possessions are important, but a life that was well lived for God is the greatest treasure handed down.

What does a real, thriving spiritual inheritance look like? There are two major pillars that hold up a true flourishing legacy:

1. Legacy is leaving something behind that will outlast you.

I've heard it said that living with legacy in mind is like planting a tree, knowing that you will never sit under its shade. Too often, we live our lives for today. A legacy plants, waters, and builds for those who will come after us. Sometimes our vision planning and mission statements for our lives and ministries are too short sighted. We make our five and ten-year plans. What would happen if we lived our lives building a foundation that the next generation could build upon? This is how David finished his life. He made plenty of mistakes, but this man—whom God described as a man after His own heart—desired more than anything to build God a house. Nearing the end of his life, he revealed all of his preparations that he had made for Solomon, his son, to build the house.

> "O Lord our God, all this abundance that we have provided for building you a house for your holy name comes from your hand and is all your own. I know, my God, that you test the heart and have pleasure in uprightness. In the uprightness of my heart I have freely offered all these things, and now I have seen your people, who are present here, offering freely and joyously to you. O Lord, the God of Abraham, Isaac, and Israel, our fathers, keep forever such purposes and thoughts in the hearts of your people, and direct their hearts toward you. Grant to Solomon my son a whole heart that he may keep your commandments,

your testimonies, and your statutes, performing all, and that he
may build the palace for which I have made provision."

—1 CHRONICLES 29:16–19

David had spent a good portion of his life saving up so that his son
would have the privilege of building God's house. The temple of Solomon
would be one of the most spectacular wonders the world would ever see.
David didn't just leave him the finances and the materials to build it. More
importantly, he left a pattern of love for the Lord that Solomon could
follow. Now this was a legacy!

I look back on my own life, and I am grateful for the legacy of faith
that my grandparents have given to me. Married for sixty-eight years and
faithfully serving the Lord, they established the pattern for me to watch
and follow after.

What if we each determined we were going to do everything in our
power to leave behind a stronger, healthier church for the next generation? What if we sacrificially invested our hard-earned resources into
building beautiful sanctuaries because we had a vision of our great-great-
grandchildren getting married in them? To do this, we need to have a
perspective shift.

2. Legacy is not leaving just something *for* people; it's leaving something *in* people.

The real fruit of our life is measured and defined by the people we
impact. The things that we buy may last for a century, but the investment we make into others will last for eternity. One of my favorite quotes
of all time is from the movie *The Gladiator*. Maximus, a Roman general,
standing before his troops attempting to motivate them for the ensuing
battle, stirs them by shouting, "Brothers, what we do in life echoes in
eternity!"[1]

Jesus taught us that, if we are wise, we will invest in the spiritual and
eternal. The only things that are eternal are things connected to people
and the things that connect people to the kingdom of God. Our time,
money, and talents all have an expiration date on them, but when they
are invested into things for the kingdom's sake, a spiritual exchange takes
place. Our investment becomes an eternal legacy.

"Do not lay up for yourselves treasures on earth, where moth and rust destroy and where thieves break in and steal, but lay up for yourselves treasure in heaven, where neither moth nor rust destroys and where thieves do not break in and steal. For where your treasure is, there your heart will be also."

—MATTHEW 6:19–21

Jesus is talking about legacy. We can leave an indelible mark on others that outlives us because it continues to live in them. This is what Jesus demonstrated by investing into twelve men who were forever changed because of His deposit. Paul followed the same pattern and left a legacy to his spiritual son, Timothy.

You, however, have followed my teaching, my conduct, my aim in life, my faith, my patience, my love, my steadfastness, my persecutions and sufferings that happened to me at Antioch, at Iconium, and at Lystra—what persecutions I endured; yet from them all the Lord rescued me.

—2 TIMOTHY 3:10–11

We all stand on the shoulders of these giants in the faith. We've read their testimonies, and they have strengthened us and given us the faith to believe for the impossible. We owe the next generation a legacy of faith and testimonies of God's faithfulness to spur them on as we have been.

A Generation Distracted

We live in a time unlike any other when it comes to distractions and competition for our time and attention. We still have the same twenty-four hours a day, but the number of things competing for our energy is exponentially greater than any generation before us. Along with that come the decisions we make about where we will invest our lives. Many times, we become victims of the urgent or swept away by the current of what everybody else is doing around us. This can leave us living lives that are busy but not necessarily fruitful.

So many even in the church have become duped into seeing the church as something other than our legacy environment. We spend immeasurable amounts of money and time on things like sports and recreation. We meticulously plan out our retirement portfolios and allow the best of our lives to be consumed by the temporal. Without our being aware, a Trojan horse has made its way into the way we think. It is the lie that says, "Church is optional" or "Church is outdated." If we believe this lie, we will become laborers in other fields that do not yield kingdom legacies.

If we could gain the revelation of the house of God as the spiritual soil that our lives were designed by God to thrive in, not only would we experience the joy of living flourishing, green, and spiritually fulfilled lives, but we would also leave a compounded blessing to the next generation as we shout from the banisters of heaven as part of that great cloud of witnesses. Only eternity will put things into the proper perspective. I'm reminded of the words of Psalm 84:10:

> For a day in your courts is better than a thousand elsewhere.
> I would rather be a doorkeeper in the house of my God than dwell in the tents of wickedness.

An Invitation to Flourish

I believe the best days of the church are still ahead of us. Despite the devil's strategies to diminish the value of church, to distract the saints, and to destroy our effectiveness, God is building a church that, like Jesus said, the gates of Hades shall not prevail against (Matthew 16:18). God is moving in unprecedented ways around the globe, and He is preparing a bride. When He comes back, He isn't coming back to rescue a few, rag-tag leftovers who are beat up and discouraged. He's coming back for a powerful church, full of men and women from every nation and generation, who are flourishing in unity and anointing and who are seeing the greatest harvest the world has ever witnessed.

The prophet Isaiah prophesied God's intentions for the church, the house of the Lord, in the latter days:

> It shall come to pass in the latter days that the mountain of the house of the Lord shall be established as the highest of the mountains, and shall be lifted up above the hills; and all the nations shall flow to it, and many peoples shall come, and say: "Come, let us go up to the mountain of the Lord, to the house

of the God of Jacob, that he may teach us his ways and that we may walk in his paths." For out of Zion shall go forth the law, and the word of the Lord from Jerusalem.

—Isaiah 2:1–3

You were created to thrive and flourish. You were designed in such a way that the spiritually charged atmosphere of God's house would activate the identity, intimacy, and destiny woven into your spiritual DNA.

Can you see yourself flourishing in all that God has created you to be? Can you look out in front of you and, instead of being alone, can you see yourself fully fitted and fully loved in a spiritual family? Can you picture yourself living out the rest of your life bearing fruit that brings praise and glory to God for eternity? What do you see when you consider what it means for you to be a disciple of Jesus Christ in the midst of a world gone crazy? Are you barely surviving, or are you thriving, strong and full of the power and purpose of God? This is what you were created for, and this is worth pursuing.

For everything that God created, He made a corresponding environment for it to reach its maximum potential and live out its purpose. Whenever a seed finds the right soil and climate, the future begins to unfold and the promise of multiplication starts to take shape. God has an environment for you. It's His house.

You were made to be a part of what God is doing in the earth as part of His family.

I hope that, as you have read these pages, you have heard the invitation of the Holy Spirit to sink deep roots into the house of God. He wants you to become rooted and grounded in the midst of a world gone wrong, so you can flourish and be fruitful. I hope you have not only heard this invitation but that you would also respond to it with a resounding yes! I pray that we would be left in awe and wonder the way Jacob was when he received the revelation of God's house:

> Surely the Lord is in this place, and I did not know it.... How awesome is this place! This is none other than the house of God, and this is the gate of heaven.
>
> —Genesis 28:16–17

NOTES

Chapter One

1. Jayalakshmi K., "African Plant Points to Diamond Bearing Kimberlite in Soil," *International Business Times Online*, May 7, 2015, https://www.ibtimes.co.uk/african-plant-points-diamond-bearing-kimberlite-soil-1500081.

Chapter Two

1. "Jacob meaning," Abarim Publications, http://www.abarim-publications.com/Meaning/Jacob.html#.XSzs2JNKhhE.
2. "Luz meaning," Abarim Publications, http://www.abarim-publications.com/Meaning/Luz.html#.XE8ya89KhhE.
3. T. J. VanderWeele, "Religion and Health: a Synthesis," *Spirituality and Religion within the Culture of Medicine: From Evidence to Practice* (New York, NY: Oxford University Press, 2017), https://pik.fas.harvard.edu/files/pik/files/chapter.pdf.
4. Gallup, "How Millenials Want to Work and Live," Gallup.com, 2016, https://enviableworkplace.com/wp-content/uploads/Gallup-How-Millennials-Want-To-Work.pdf.
5. David Noel Freedman, ed., *Eerdmans Dictionary of the Bible* (Grand Rapids, MI: W.B. Eerdmans, 2000), 236.
6. Derek Kidner, *Genesis: An Introduction and Commentary* (Downers Grove, IL: InterVarsity Press, 1967), 132.
7. Melissa Steffan, "An Inside Look at Church Attenders that Tithe the Most: A New State of the Plate Report Finds Surprising Generosity and Financial Health Among Top Tithers," *Christianity Today*, May 17, 2013, https://www.christianitytoday.com/news/2013/may/inside-look-at-church-attenders-who-tithe-most.html.

Chapter Three

1. Ishan Daftardar, "Scientific Analysis of Michael Phelps's Body Structure," ScienceABC.com, www.scienceabc.com/sports/michael-phelps-height-arms-torso-arm-span-feet-swimming.html.
2. Wilhelm Gesenius and Samuel Prideaux Tregelles, *Gesenius' Hebrew and Chaldee Lexicon to the Old Testament Scriptures* (Bellingham, WA: Logos Bible Software, 2003), 758.
3. James E. Smith, ed., *Theological Wordbook of the Old Testament* (Chicago: Moody Press, 1999), 168.

Chapter Four

1. Caleb Culver, Cory Asbury, and Ran Jackson, "Reckless Love," Essential Music Publishing, Bethel Music, Watershed Music Group, 2018. Lyric reprint permission given by Essential Music Publishing and Watershed Music Group.

Chapter Six

1. Dick Drewsbury, "Family Reunited with Amnesia-Suffering Father 23 Years After His Burned Out Car was Found and He Vanished," DailyMail. com, August, 13, 2012, https://www.dailymail.co.uk/news/article-2187627 /Family-reunited-amnesia-suffering-father-23-years-burned-car-vanished.html.

Chapter Seven

1. Merriam-Webster.com, s.v. "community," https://www.merriam-webster .com/dictionary/community.

2. Walter A. Elwell and Barry J. Beitzel, *Baker Encyclopedia of the Bible* (Grand Rapids, MI: Baker Book House, 1988), 488, s.v. "church."

3. Spiros Zodhiates, ThD, *The Complete Wordstudy Dictionary: New Testament* (Chattanooga, TN: AMG Publishers, 2000).

Chapter Ten

1. Ridley Scott, *Gladiator* (DreamWorks, Glendale, CA, 2010).